insight text guide

Sue Tweg

Othello

William Shakespeare

First published in 2001, reprinted 2002–2010, 2012, 2013, 2014, 2015, 2016, 2017, 2018, 2019 (twice), 2020, 2021, 2022.

Insight Publications Pty Ltd
3/350 Charman Road
Cheltenham VIC 3192
Australia
Tel: +61 3 8571 4950
Fax: +61 3 8571 0257
Email: books@insightpublications.com.au

www.insightpublications.com.au

National Library of Australia Cataloguing-in-Publication entry:
Tweg, Sue
William Shakespeare's Othello: text guide
For secondary and tertiary students.
9781875882359 (pbk.)
1. Shakespeare, William, 1564-1616. Othello. I. Title.
(Series : Insight text guide).
822.33

Other ISBNs:
9781922378408 (digital)
9781922378415 (bundle: print + digital)

Cover design: The Modern Art Production Group

Printed in Australia by Ligare

contents

CHARACTER MAP

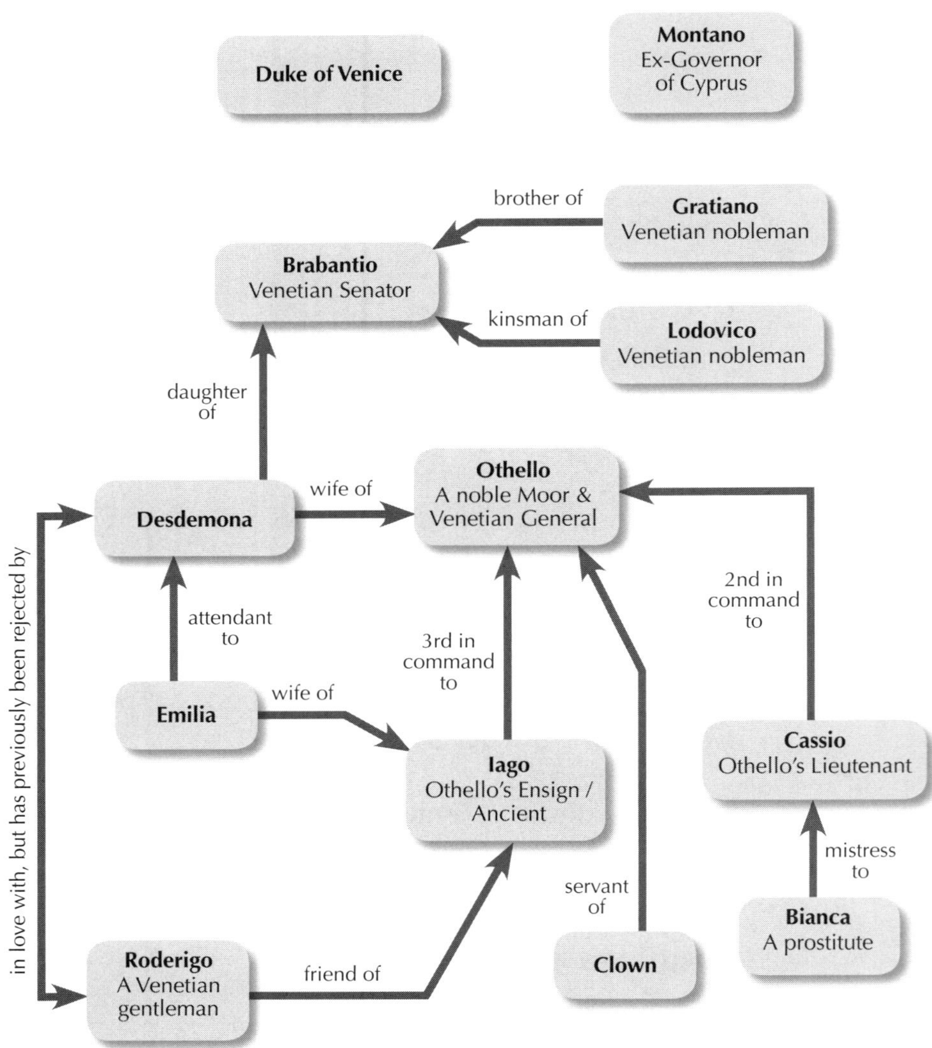

Also appearing: Herald, Officers, Gentlemen, Messenger, Sailor, musicians and various attendants

OVERVIEW

About the author

William Shakespeare is one of the most renowned literary figures from the English literary Renaissance (also referred to as the 'early modern period'). His dramatic and poetic work, written during an intensely productive period from the late-sixteenth to early-seventeenth century, has proved capable of enduring well beyond his own time and place. Translated into many languages, adapted for film, ballet, opera and graphic novels, Shakespeare's work has evolved into a cultural phenomenon, meaningful and compelling to audiences of different periods and cultures.

Shakespeare was born in 1564 when Elizabeth I was on the throne and died in 1616 when James I was king. Born in Stratford-upon-Avon, in Warwickshire, he received an education from the Stratford grammar school, but never attended university.

In the late 1580s Shakespeare moved to London and began his career as a playwright. He joined a theatre company called the Chamberlain's Men (also briefly known as Lord Hunsdon's Men), under the patronage of the Lord Chamberlain, which produced plays performed at a theatre called 'the Theatre'. He acted, wrote plays and shared in the profits of the theatre company. When the lease over the land on which the Theatre was built expired in 1597, and a dispute with the landlord arose, Shakespeare and his colleagues dismantled the wooden theatre and took it across the river Thames, reassembling the structure at Bankside, a district which was part of the Southwark borough south of the Thames. This theatre became the Globe, which opened in 1599. In London today a replica Globe now stands on the original site and Shakespeare's plays are performed here all year round.

When James I came to the throne in 1603, he became the patron of the theatre company of which Shakespeare was part owner; the company was therefore renamed as the King's Men. The king recognised the huge potential of the theatre to reach many people; the theatre can perhaps be thought of as the early-seventeenth century equivalent of television in this regard. James wanted his reign to be associated with that power, despite the fact that there is a strong critique of authority figures throughout Shakespeare's work.

Othello is one of Shakespeare's most well-known plays. This guide is designed to help you navigate your way through the play, organise your thinking and help you to write intelligently and competently on the play in your essays and exams. Remember that *Othello* is a *play*, created to be experienced as a performance on stage, even though we often first experience it as a written text, reading it alone and silently. If you are able to see the play performed you will gain a deeper understanding of its shape, the characters, how the dramatic action unfolds and the effect of Shakespeare's language. Film adaptations will also help in understanding the play, particularly watching different screen versions.

Synopsis

Shakespeare's *Othello* (like the other three great tragedies *Hamlet*, *Macbeth* and *King Lear*, which he wrote in a cluster somewhere around the years 1600 to 1606 for the actors at the Globe), is named after the central tragic protagonist, a noble man who has lived honourably up to the moment in the play when everything he understands about life changes catastrophically.

Iago, who hates Othello for his decision to promote Cassio to the rank of lieutenant instead of him, opens the action with information about a mixed-race marriage. The union, between Othello and Desdemona, has been carried out in secret, at night, because of anticipated parental disapproval. Together with Roderigo, whose love for Desdemona has gone unrequited, they wake Brabantio, the bride's father.

Othello, on his way to answer an urgent call from the senate in response to the military threat posed by Turkey to Cyprus, is intercepted by Brabantio and accused of trying to steal his daughter. It is deemed such a serious matter that the senate turn their attentions from the impending war to resolving the dispute. Despite Brabantio's misgivings, loudly aired in public, society leaders tolerate this marriage because the husband is useful to the community and the well-respected bride is articulate and determined enough to insist on being accepted as his partner. Brabantio, bitter at the senate's decision, sows the first seed of doubt in Othello's mind by warning him to beware his new bride, who has willingly deceived her own father.

Othello, accompanied by Desdemona, sails to Cyprus to help defend the island. They arrive safely, in part due to a storm which has sunk the Turkish fleet; the night is spent celebrating the victory and their marriage. After Othello and Desdemona go to bed, Cassio is left in charge. Iago's plan to usurp him becomes clear as he sets about encouraging Cassio to get drunk, before starting a brawl which he blames on the lieutenant. Othello is woken by the alarm, and trusting Iago's version of events dismisses Cassio, who remains unaware of Iago's duplicity.

The next step of Iago's plot is revealed as he suggests Cassio should ingratiate himself to Desdemona in order to win back the esteem he has lost with Othello. Meanwhile, Iago posits the idea to Othello that Cassio and Desdemona are having an affair. Presented with Desdemona's lost handkerchief as 'evidence' of the relationship, Othello instructs Iago to kill Cassio.

Othello eventually confronts Desdemona over the alleged affair; despite her protestations he smothers her with a pillow. Only after she is dead does the truth become apparent to him – his grief and guilt lead him to take his own life. Iago is exposed for the villain that he is and taken away to be tortured.

Character summaries

Othello: The moor of Venice, a noble man who has risen to the rank of General within the Venetian army despite racial prejudice.

Iago: A soldier serving Othello personally. Jealous at the advancement of others in his place, he proves to be a master of deceit.

Desdemona: Daughter of Brabantio and wife of Othello. Loyal to her husband, with whom she shares her biggest fault; naivety.

Cassio: A soldier loyal to Othello, he is tricked by Iago into playing an unwitting part in the General's downfall.

Emilia: Wife of Iago and attendant to Desdemona. She is unaware of her husband's schemes and ultimately reveals his villainy, for which he kills her.

Roderigo: A friend of Iago, he is in love with Desdemona and envies Othello. Iago eventually kills him in an effort to cover up his plans after the failed attempt on Cassio's life.

Brabantio: Desdemona's father. His advice to Othello regarding the perceived duplicity of his daughter sows the first seeds of doubt, long before Iago's plotting begins to bear fruit.

BACKGROUND & CONTEXT

Italy and Italians

Othello is set in two locations, Venice and the island of Cyprus (an important defensive outpost for the Venetian state at this time). Original playgoers would have been exposed to certain attitudes to Italy, which would have helped to colour their interpretation of this exotic story in performance. Cultural stereotypes still persist, as we know, and it is important to recognise their power to influence us, even when we know we are looking at fictional characters on a stage or onscreen.

Italy and Italian temperaments were known to ordinary English people in the sixteenth and early seventeenth centuries largely through stage representations, like the exotic bunch of characters they could see in *Shakespeare's Taming of the Shrew, Romeo and Juliet, Much Ado About Nothing, The Merchant of Venice* and *Othello*, among other plays set in different parts of a culturally and politically divided country. Some audience members would have already absorbed background information about the Catholic empires of Italy and Spain (and the classical worlds of Greece and Rome) in other ways, before they even set foot in the playhouse. Young men, for example, would have absorbed a combination of fact, recent and ancient history and classical myth through Latin texts and translations that formed the basis of their education in grammar schools. Comparatively few members of any audience would have had first-hand experience of European travel to go on, so pre-formed opinions and prejudices mattered.

People who could read in Shakespeare's time also began to acquire hot-off-the-press English or French translations of Italian prose *novellas* (these were literally 'new' short prose fiction, the beginnings of what we still call 'novels'). Here readers could find a rich descriptive mixture of corruption and vice, of love, lust, vendetta, rivalry, forced marriages, imprisonment, casual slaying, torture and every kind of cruelty and decadence, set in opulent palaces or places of religion. In just such an Italian *novella*, translated into French, Shakespeare found his source story for *Othello*, entitled *Disdemona and the Moorish Captain*.

Prejudice

Prejudiced perceptions about the 'latin temperament' still exist. An important factor shaping English views in Shakespeare's time – basically, that Italians and Spaniards were generally dangerous political and moral enemies – stemmed from the recent religious upheaval known as the Reformation, when Protestant England had formally withdrawn its religious allegiance to the Pope and Catholic Rome, and named its own monarch, Henry VIII, head of the English Church and 'Defender of the Faith'. When Henry's daughter, Queen Elizabeth, ruled during Shakespeare's lifetime, Italian and Spanish visitors to England were likely to be viewed with deep suspicion as both decadent heretics and potential assassins. Plays featuring Italian and Spanish characters were therefore viewed with particular interest – despite the presence of honourable Venetians in the story, Iago confirmed playgoers' worst expectations.

Machiavelli

Furthermore, the name of the Florentine Niccolò Machiavelli (1469–1527) was widely known as a byword for cynicism and diabolical cunning: knowing quite well that the theatre audience would understand what he meant, Shakespeare's character Richard Duke of Gloucester (soon to be the monstrous Richard III) alluded to Machiavelli when he claimed he could teach 'the murderous Machevil' a thing or two about being a villain (*Henry VI*, 3.2.193).

Italian women in Shakespeare's time

If Italian men were viewed stereotypically in Shakespeare's time as potentially dangerous schemers, Italian women – especially Venetian women – were notorious by repute as a pack of prostitutes. Storr (1989) quotes late sixteenth-century estimates for types of women in Venice: 2,889 upper-class ladies, 2,508 nuns, 1,936 burgher women, and 11,654 courtesans. Iago's wife, Emilia, is certainly a freethinker about sex, in contrast to Desdemona's chaste but playful erotic imagination, but there is no evidence to suggest that Shakespeare is portraying either of these women as whorish, whatever their husbands suspect about them. On the other hand, Cassio's mistress, Bianca, is clearly a working girl selling sexual favours. The issue of how Shakespeare portrays female sexuality in the play, given contemporary popular ideas about Italian women, is discussed further. (See Themes, Ideas & Values, p.48.)

Venice

The Venetian state was known to the people of Shakespeare's time as a great trading nation and sea power. It had been engaged in a battle with the Turkish empire (Christian against Muslim) for control of Mediterranean territory and seaways since the early fifteenth century. Cyprus had been added to the Venetian state in 1489 and was an important garrison island, before passing finally into Turkey's hands in 1573 as part of a peace settlement.

Othello's background

Othello is therefore set in the period before 1573, when Venice and Cyprus are under military threat: General Othello, Ancient [Ensign] Iago and Lieutenant Cassio are all veterans of campaigns against the Turks, so it is good policy to appoint Othello governor of Cyprus in the crisis. Othello himself is a Moor (and therefore Muslim), who has converted to Christianity after settling in Italy. How he got to Venice from his home in North Africa is not certain, although he hints at the dangers and adventures he has known, including a period of slavery, in his long speech to the senators in Act I Scene 3, 127–169.

Shakespeare's theatre

Othello was performed in 1604 before the new king, James I, at the Banqueting House, Whitehall, and again in 1612 for a royal wedding. This was an elegant indoor space, with candles to light the performance, a band of musicians and an invited courtly audience. But Shakespeare's plays, including Othello, were more frequently performed in the Globe, a public open-air theatre on the south bank of the Thames. Here conditions were different: all performances took place in broad daylight, scenery and props (like beds and candles for *Othello*) were minimal. A large stage jutted out into the audience, which was made up of a representative cross-section of London society of both sexes, from the wealthy to the relatively poor. Actors had to train their voices to be able to reach every audience member in the large wooden 'O' shape of the theatre, a space that could accommodate over three thousand people. Actors also knew that they had to rely on language to create the atmosphere for a scene, to help the audience imagine details of weather conditions, temperature and the time of day or night. There are a number of good websites which show the re-constructed Globe Theatre.

GENRE, STRUCTURE & LANGUAGE

Tragedy

The term 'tragedy', first applied to describe Classical Greek theatre, defines the kind of serious play that deliberately arouses, as Aristotle argued, our '*pleasure* of pity and fear' for the tragic protagonist (Abrams 1988, 189–193, my emphasis). This protagonist is neither a complete villain nor a saint but a noble man (or, much less often, a woman) with a mixture of faults and virtues. While we are led to pity him, we also experience fear because we recognise our life could just as easily be destroyed through similar faults as this noble example who is 'better than we are' to begin with. When the hero finally encounters the reversal of fortune (Greek *peripeteia*) followed by *catastrophe*, partly through his own pride (Greek *hubris*) or an error of judgement (Greek *hamartia*, the 'fatal flaw'), Aristotle argued that we experience a pleasurable release of tension, accompanied by a sense of relief that balance has somehow been restored to the world through a kind of cleansing, or purging, of the fault (Greek *catharsis*). This is Aristotle's basic idea of how tragedy works.

Shakespearean tragedies do seem to close by bringing to an end the disruptive elements that have led to the catastrophe, although there is sometimes a lingering sense that cosmic order has been restored only temporarily. *Othello* certainly ends with calm but at a terrible price: the final moments onstage reveal Othello, Desdemona and Emilia dead, Iago wounded, Cassio maimed and the Venetian lords shocked into silence.

Shakespearean tragedy

Othello is a tragedy, which means that its noble protagonist is likely to be undermined by circumstances, combined with some 'fatal flaw' in his own personality. In Shakespeare's other great tragedies we could say that for Hamlet, the fatal flaw is hesitation, for Macbeth it is uncontrollable ambition, and for King Lear emotional blindness. Othello's fatal flaw is, as he realises too late, that he has been *'one that loved not wisely, but too well'* (5.2.340), bringing horror into his own peaceful life by trusting the wrong person.

But this is too simplistic. Shakespeare gives his great tragic characters much more complex motivations, so that what you've just read above reduces the psychological and emotional struggles of an intelligent person to a single character 'flaw'. What is Othello's 'flaw'? Is he too trusting? Yes, he is. Or is his ego too easily bruised, so that he becomes instantly offended when he thinks his honour has been attacked? Yes, again – but even this is only half true. Is he anxious about sex? We could certainly guess so, from his excited response to Iago's hints, but again he has good reason to feel anxious, as well. And worried about being black in a white society? Yes, he refers to this more than once – but again he has some justification. We need to take time to work out a subtle reading of Othello's personality. He isn't a single-minded tragic hero who is cut down by events, nor a jealous wife-killer, but one who calls himself at the end an *'honourable murderer'* (5.2. 291).

Shakespearean tragedy works on the principle that protagonists are not able to see the whole picture of their circumstances until the very end of their lives, although information is revealed to the audience throughout the play. We therefore feel frustrated sorrow because we can only watch as they keep making the wrong decisions or mistake the truth or, like Othello, are led deeper into confusion by the one person they listen to. Their collapse and demise is not just personal tragedy, either – it affects the people they love, their friends and their country. Tragedy, as Shakespeare writes it, is about the huge ripple effect of the individual's collapse. And as the Prince says at the end of *Romeo and Juliet*, ultimately *'All are punish'd'* (5.3.295) by the catastrophe that overwhelms the protagonist.

Style and language

The play is constructed in two main language styles. Mostly it reads as the familiar Shakespearean blank verse (unrhymed iambic pentameter lines), illustrated, for example, when you listen to the five stresses per line and easy rhythm of formal English speech in a few lines from Desdemona's speech to the Senate (1.3.245–9):

> That I did love the Moor to live with him,
> My downright violence and storm of fortunes
> May trumpet to the world. My heart's subdued
> Even to the very quality of my lord.
> I saw Othello's visage in his mind ...

I have underlined the five stresses I'd make in each line. Notice that they don't have to make a sing-song regular pattern to keep the poetic line moving. Iambic pentameter verse still holds its basic structure when a conversation is going on that breaks up lines between speakers and this is an important cue for actors about the way characters are interacting. For instance, in the following example lines fragment under the tension of a fraught moment between Iago and Othello (4.1.23):

> IAGO: Ay, what of that?
> OTHELLO: That's not so good now.
> IAGO: What
> If I had said, I had seen him do you wrong ...

Iago frequently switches to the vernacular (everyday prose speech), as you can see by the change in line patterns on the printed page, for example when he is speaking to Roderigo about 'virtue' in 1.3 or in his aside 2.1.164–173. Breaking into prose adds a sense of urgency to Iago's words but also lets us recognise that he's stepped out of the poetic dramatic frame for a moment – he's talking like an ordinary person. Prose marks him as more 'common' than the characters who habitually speak in verse. Cassio speaks prose when he's drunk (2.3) and Bianca the prostitute speaks prose to Cassio (4.1).

Tone

These stylistic shifts move the tone of the language through a wide range of possibilities from heroic-sounding to lyrical, from mystical to sordid, from noble perceptions to the banality of the everyday. Find some examples of these tonal differences in the iambic pentameter verse.

Metaphor and poetry

Othello is often considered to be Shakespeare's most 'poetic' play and it is rich in metaphor. Notice how the language creates a whole spectrum of word pictures in its imagery, from incredible beauty to appalling ugliness. Look for animal imagery, plant and garden imagery, allusions to jewels and precious objects, allusions to heaven and hell, damnation, devils and angels, storm and sea imagery. See what other recurrent ideas you can find.

Structure

Othello was printed first in 1622, then again for the Folio of 1623, several years after Shakespeare's death: the formal division into five acts, each with several scenes, was clearly the manuscript editor's decision. As you study the play, remember that stage directions, too, are usually modern editorial insertions which should be considered as suggestions for staging but need not be slavishly followed.

The action of the play moves swiftly from Venice to Cyprus, from emotional harmony to chaos, from Othello's marriage and civic triumph to his death and apparent fall from grace. Critics have argued about the logistical impossibility of Desdemona being unfaithful to Othello (can't he see that she would have had no time?) or the speed with which events occur in Cyprus (has Othello's marriage even been consummated, for instance?) In performance, the need for an apparent 'double time scheme' to make Iago's suggestions plausible, let alone for all the comings and goings from Venice, hardly seems worth worrying about because we simply make allowances for dramatic necessity.

SCENE-BY-SCENE ANALYSIS

The following synopsis highlights **key scenes** in the play.

Act 1

Scene 1

Summary: *Night, in the street outside Brabantio's house. Establishes Iago's and Roderigo's characters. We learn about Othello's secret marriage to Desdemona, Brabantio's daughter.*

Iago, a discontented soldier serving Othello, encourages Roderigo, a rich fool lusting for Desdemona, to provide him with money to act as an intercessor – even though Roderigo strikes us immediately as an unattractive suitor to any woman. Roderigo whines to Iago about not being told of Desdemona's secret marriage to Othello. It seems that Iago has been caught out, too. His hatred for Othello becomes apparent, together with an admission that his outward friendliness to the Moor is false: 'I am not what I am' (1.1.66). Iago incites Roderigo to stir up Desdemona's father, Brabantio, although he, Iago, does most of the shouting, describing Desdemona and Othello loudly to Brabantio in gross sexual terms – 'your daughter and the Moor are now making the beast with two backs' (p.116).

Key quote

Iago: Though I do hate him (Othello) as I do hell pains,
Yet for necessity of present life
I must show out a flag and sign of love
Which is indeed but sign.

(1.1.155–158)

Key point

This scene reveals **Iago's** character quickly. He professes to be a more suitable Lieutenant for Othello than Cassio whom he dismisses as 'a great arithmetician, ... a Florentine ... a bookish theoric' whose soldiership is 'mere prattle without practice'. Note how he constantly describes Othello in derogatory terms: 'his Moorship, the Moor'. He tells Brabantio that Othello is 'an old black ram tupping your white ewe' (Desdemona) (89–90) and that Brabantio will have his daughter 'covered by a Barbary (country on north coast of Africa and therefore black) horse' (112). He crudely says 'your daughter and the Moor are now making the beast with two backs' (117). His true attitude to Othello is hate: 'I do hate him as I do hell pains'; but his deceptive nature: 'I am not what I am' (66); requires that 'for necessity ... I must show out a flag and sign of love (to Othello)'. He incites Roderigo to insult Othello to Brabantio as 'a knave of common hire, a gondolier (126), ... a lascivious Moor (127), ... an extravagant and wheeling stranger' (137).

Scene 2

Summary: *Othello's first appearance. Iago joins Othello in the street. Cassio brings news that the Duke urgently seeks Othello as warnings from Cyprus suggest threats from Turkey. Brabantio arrives and accuses Othello of stealing his daughter.*

Iago joins Othello, walking in the night street. Despite Iago's description of Brabantio's rage, Othello remains calm and unafraid, in control of the situation. Because he is the state's foremost General, he is summoned urgently to the Duke's council of war. Then, confronted by Brabantio, who accuses him of practicing witchcraft on Desdemona, Othello agrees to justify his marriage before the Duke.

Key quote

Othello: For know, Iago,
But that I love the gentle Desdemona.

(1.2.24–25)

Note Othello's openness and trust in his reputation and also Iago's reference to Janus and its significance.

Key points

This scene introduces **Othello** and shows his trusting attitude to Iago.

Othello shows his level-headedness when accused by Brabantio of stealing his daughter. He uses calm and reason to deflect Brabantio's order that he go to prison: 'What if I do obey? / How may the Duke be ... satisfied?' (1.2.87–88).

Scene 3

Summary: *There are three distinct parts to this scene: a discussion of the Turkish threat and Othello's bravery as a soldier (1.3.1–46); Othello's defence of his marriage against Brabantio's accusations with Desdemona's support and presence (1.3.48–297); Iago's duplicity – he leads Roderigo on to believe he can win Desdemona; he is hatching a plot that will make Othello think Cassio is 'too familiar with his wife' (1.3.298–398).*

At the Duke's Council of War, Turkey's threats to Cyprus, Venice's prized possession, are confirmed. However, Brabantio interrupts with cries of grief about his 'stolen' daughter. Othello admits the marriage and presents his case, calling on Desdemona to state clearly for herself that he was her husband of choice. They appear together in public and we see how they interact as a loving, cooperative pair. Othello appears before the Duke in a double role; as alien seducer according to Desdemona's father and as a trusted Venetian military leader.

Othello's speech about his past life *is* seductive – it certainly wins over the Duke to support the marriage. Desdemona repudiates her father politely in public, asking to be allowed to accompany Othello on the military expedition to Cyprus. Brabantio's last words to Othello are a warning that he should keep an eye on Desdemona: '*She has deceived her father and may thee*' (1.3.290).

Left alone onstage, Iago has to persuade the feeble Roderigo not to give up hope, arguing that the marriage '*between an erring barbarian and a super-subtle Venetian*' (351) is so unnatural that it is bound to fail. By the end of the scene, Iago reveals in soliloquy that he has worked out part of his plot to destroy Othello's happiness.

Key quotes

Othello: Honest Iago
My Desdemona must I leave to thee.

(1.3.291–292)

Iago: The Moor is of a free and open nature,
That thinks men honest that but seem to be so,
And will as tenderly be led by th'nose
As asses are.

(1.3.393–396)

Key points

Note the **Duke's** and **Senator's** references to 'the valiant Moor, valiant Othello' (1.3.48),' brave Moor' (1.3.288) contrast with Iago's attacks on Othello's character. How has Iago in Act I made it possible for the audience to believe Othello's honesty and integrity?

Note **Brabantio's** extreme (racist?) reaction to Desdemona's marriage: 'She is abused, stolen from me, and corrupted / By spells and medicines ...' (1.3.60–61) which he concludes must be 'witchcraft'.

His behaviour alerts us to the patriarchal expectations of the day – a daughter obeys her father and remains with him and supportive of him until she marries – according to *his* wishes.

Othello once again puts faith in his own good name, calling on Desdemona to speak for herself.

His integrity in his account of their love and how he won her heart shines through: 'She loved me for the dangers I had passed, / And I loved her, that she did pity them' (1.3.166–167). His arguments and his honesty refute Brabantio's attacks and establish his trustworthiness with both the Senators and the audience.

Desdemona makes her first appearance (1.3.169). Note how she addresses her father, 'My noble father, I do perceive here a divided duty' (1.3.179), in directly identifying the issue, acknowledging her duty which now is 'Due to the Moor, my lord' (1.3.187). Look closely at her direct but respectful language, her conciliatory but assertive tone throughout.

Q **Othello** accepts **Iago**, his Ancient (Ensign; a flag bearer) as 'A man ... of honesty and trust' – so much so that he entrusts his wife to his care. What is your reaction to Othello's trusting attitude towards Iago?

Q **Iago's** hatred fires his dastardly plan to make **Othello** suspect **Cassio** of being 'too familiar with his wife'. 'Hell and night / Must bring this monstrous birth to the world's light' (397–398). Why do you think Iago is obsessed with bringing about Othello's downfall? Is it hatred? Evil? Racial prejudice? Jealousy? What evidence do you have so far to support your view?

Act 2

Scene 1

Summary: *The action moves to Cyprus, where a fierce storm has delivered the Venetian army victory over the Turks. Othello and Desdemona speak of their love and happiness.*

Key scene

In Cyprus, members of the garrison who wait anxiously for the Venetian ships to come through the storm show their concern for Othello's safety. This scene shows Desdemona's innocence, the high regard in which Othello is held, his unsuspecting trust of Iago and Iago's continued devilish plots.

The soldiers express their admiration for Othello as a noble soldier. Cassio arrives first, with happy news of Othello's marriage. Then Iago, his wife Emilia and Desdemona arrive safely. While they wait for Othello's ship, the women and Iago pass the time by talking about female virtues and vices. Iago notices Cassio's fondness for Desdemona and sees an opportunity for further mischief-making. Finally, Othello arrives safely to be embraced by Desdemona. Roderigo is enraged by their show of affection but Iago again placates him by working up lecherous ideas to ruin the lovers. In the final important soliloquy Iago admits love for Desdemona and jealousy of Othello.

Key quotes

Othello: (Re-united with Desdemona) If I were now to die,
'Twere now to be most happy.

(2.1.183–184)

Iago: Knavery's plain face is never seen till used.

(2.1.304)

Key points

Desdemona and Othello's mutual love further incites Iago to plot their downfall. Both Roderigo and Cassio suit his purposes well – Roderigo because he is so easily persuaded despite his own observations about Desdemona's nature and the innocence of her social exchanges with Cassio. Iago's persuasive tongue quickly dupes him. For example, courtesy is dismissed as lechery (248–249); Cassio's obvious but innocent affection for Desdemona is particularly useful to Iago's schemes.

Iago grows more villainous in this scene; note especially the final soliloquy in which he tells the audience his true motives.

Scene 2

Summary: *A herald announces that Othello has commanded a night of feasting to celebrate his nuptial (i.e. for his wedding night).*

Scene 3

Summary: *Othello goes to bed with Desdemona, leaving Cassio in command. Iago gets Cassio drunk and instigates a fight between him and Roderigo. Othello wakes and blames Cassio, dismissing him from the rank of Lieutenant.*

Key scene

Othello orders Cassio to act as guard on his wedding night. Basically this scene sees Iago further his plans to undermine Othello by exploiting Cassio's weakness for drink; he fights and loses his position of lieutenant in a hasty decision from Othello. Iago then encourages him to seek Desdemona's help and plans to use her kindness to Cassio to arouse Othello's suspicions of her possible infidelity.

Othello leaves Cassio in charge of the night guard and Iago seizes his opportunity to exploit Cassio's 'fatal flaw' (no head for drink). Roderigo provokes Cassio into a drunken brawl, stage-managed by Iago, during which the Governor of Cyprus, Montano, is badly injured. The disturbance causes Othello to leave his wedding bed. Hearing the apparent facts, he dismisses Cassio for drunkenness and promotes Iago to Cassio's position as lieutenant. Alone with Iago, Cassio grieves for his lost *'reputation'*. Iago's comfort is laced with contempt for such a useless virtue: he advises Cassio to approach Desdemona as an intercessor, calculating in a soliloquy (2.3.326–352) how he will use the innocent relationship to arouse Othello's jealousy.

Key quote

Iago: I had rather have this tongue cut from my mouth
Than it should do offence to Michael Cassio.

(3.2.215–216) (*Note his lies and duplicity*)

Key points

Othello continues to trust Iago. What effects are gained by having the audience informed of Iago's scheming?

What is your attitude to Iago by the end of this scene? How is the character made convincing?

We see here how a trusting person accepts appearances as reality and how easily someone can manipulate weaker beings to his own ends. Discuss how the themes of reality and illusion and villainy are developing through characters' behaviour.

Choose the most apt of these words to describe Iago at this stage of the drama: scheming, clever, deceitful, crafty, sly, perfidious, Machiavellian, treacherous.

How would you describe Othello at this point in the play?

Act 3

Scene 1

Summary: *Cassio has arranged for musicians to play a morning greeting (an aubade) to the newly married couple. Emilia, Iago's wife and Desdemona's servant, tells Cassio that Desdemona and Othello have spoken of him and it seems likely that soon he will be restored to favour.*

Scene 2

Summary: *In the morning, General Othello gives orders to Iago (now his right-hand man) and sets about checking the island's fortifications.*

Scene 3

Key scene

In the first part of this long scene that builds in intensity, Cassio meets Desdemona to thank her but leaves in embarrassment as Othello appears with Iago. From this point on, Iago sows the seeds of suspicion in Othello's mind so successfully that Othello changes from loving Desdemona in complete trust to believing that she has betrayed him and should be murdered.

After Cassio's hurried exit, Iago seizes the opportunity to plant the first seeds of suspicion in Othello's mind, with a simple 'Ha! I like not that' (3.3.35). Othello remains unperturbed, even showing restrained amusement at Desdemona's playful nagging about Cassio. When she finally leaves, Othello articulates the strength of his love and has to be recalled to reality by Iago's apparently polite enquiry about Cassio.

The next 200 lines demonstrate the subtlety of Iago's insinuations, where all he needs are a few significant pauses and echoed words and phrases to poison Othello's trust in his wife. Having succeeded in his ploy, Iago leaves Othello alone onstage to soliloquise about the unsuitability of his marriage (3.3.255–274). Desdemona's appearance seems to reconfirm Othello's belief in her faithfulness – especially when she innocently tries to cure the pain in his forehead (Shakespeare's audience would immediately catch the implication of cuckold's horns) by binding it with her handkerchief. This is a crucial moment in the action because Iago's wife Emilia is present when Desdemona drops the handkerchief, more concerned to get Othello indoors to rest than pick up the object that was his first love gift to her. As they leave, Iago enters.

Emilia and Iago

The scene now focuses briefly on the relationship between Emilia and Iago. As a husband, Iago is cold – Emilia has stolen the handkerchief she knows has significance to Desdemona simply to please him but he takes it without thanks and orders her to go. In a brief soliloquy before Othello returns, Iago reveals that he wants the handkerchief to incriminate Cassio and fire Othello's jealous suspicions further.

Iago and Othello

The scene ends with a fierce exchange between Othello, overwhelmed with such violent passion that his very identity is being stripped away by what he suspects is Desdemona's infidelity, and Iago, who (possessing the mystical handkerchief) now has the means of providing *'the ocular proof'* (3.3.357) Othello demands.

Iago invents a story of Cassio's talking in his sleep, then says he's seen Cassio using Desdemona's handkerchief. Othello makes Iago swear to kill Cassio and vows to execute Desdemona himself. In a gesture of supreme hypocrisy, Iago kneels to dedicate himself to serve Othello as a real 'lieutenant' – ready to commit murder at his master's command. This scene ends with Othello resolved to find 'some swift means of death / For the fair devil' (3.3.475) and Iago vowing to Othello 'I am your own for ever' (3.3.477).

Key quotes

Iago: O, beware, my lord, of jealousy!
It is the green-eyed monster, which doth mock
The meat it feeds on.

(3.3.164–166)

Othello: All my fond love thus do I blow to heaven:
'Tis gone.
Arise, black vengeance, from thy hollow cell!
Yield up, O love, thy crown and hearted throne
To tyrannous hate!

(3.3.442–447)

Key points

Words like 'honest', 'jealous', 'think', 'know' start circling about repetitively from now on between Othello and Iago. Notice the echo effects in the language – and how crucial pauses can be.

Scene 4 – The 'handkerchief' scene

Summary: *The missing handkerchief is assuming significance that Desdemona cannot see; she unwittingly further increases Othello's suspicions that Iago has worked so cunningly to arouse; Othello's attitude and behaviour towards her completely change.*

Key scene

Desdemona, accompanied by Emilia, is looking for her lost handkerchief but is confident that Othello will not be moved to any 'ill-thinking' by its loss (3.4.29). To her surprise, Othello insists on seeing the handkerchief, explaining its magical significance at length, while Desdemona, unaware of the fatal significance of the connection, tries to force the conversation back to Cassio. Desdemona then reveals that, because 'My lord (Othello) is not my lord', Cassio will have to be patient. Iago offers to see why Othello is angry and leaves. Desdemona discusses with Emilia her innocence – 'I never gave him cause' (3.4.154) and prays that 'Heaven keep that monster (jealousy) from Othello's mind' (3.4.159).

Then, casually, Cassio meets his own mistress Bianca (a courtesan) and gives her the pretty handkerchief he found in his room to copy. Bianca expresses her jealous suspicions about the handkerchief.

Key quote

Emilia: But jealous souls will not be answered so;
They are not ever jealous for the cause,
But jealous for they're jealous. It is a monster
Begot upon itself, born on itself.

(3.4.155–158)

Key points

Desdemona is puzzled by Othello's 'strange unquietness' and Emilia is now feeling guilty about her role in the loss of the handkerchief.

Note how Othello skilfully weaves the story of its special powers to keep a couple loving and happy (55–76) so that Desdemona is powerfully affected, even though she continues to try to deflect the conversation to Cassio's problems.

This is a good example of dramatic irony – a moment where we know the truth of something that the characters onstage do not, so they jump to false conclusions. In this case, Desdemona's handkerchief finding its way into Cassio's possession will seem to verify Othello's jealous assumptions about his wife and Cassio – just as Bianca instantly assumes that the handkerchief belongs to some rival mistress of

Cassio's. The agents of all this mistaking (who *we* know about, but the characters don't) are, of course, Iago and Emilia.

Act 4

Scene 1

Summary: *Othello reveals that he still loves Desdemona despite his resolve to kill her: he is torn between that love and Iago's efforts to convince him of Desdemona's infidelity, something that seems confirmed by 'the evidence' of the handkerchief. At the end of this scene, Othello strikes the innocent Desdemona, losing the respect of the Venetians who think he must be mad.*

Key scene

Othello's poetic language now fragments in exchanges that are barely conversation, more like cues or prompts from Iago which Othello repeats, each time filling in the inference about the 'handkerchief'. Under the pressure of Iago's insistent hinting, Othello falls into an epileptic fit (the second one he's had in two days, according to Iago 4.1.51).

At this crucial moment Cassio appears. His impulse is to touch Othello but Iago keeps him at a distance. When Othello recovers, Iago orchestrates a conversation with Cassio, which Othello can see but, with Iago's contrivance, is out of earshot. Iago then makes Cassio joke about Bianca, while Othello imagines they are laughing about Desdemona. Bianca herself appears in a jealous rage to return the unknown 'love token' handkerchief to Cassio. Seeing the distinctive embroidery, Othello is convinced. Nonetheless, Iago still has to work to harden Othello's heart towards Desdemona, whose beauty and sweetness still dominates his perceptions. Iago persuades Othello to agree to kill Desdemona that night and promises that he will personally undertake to kill Cassio.

At the end of this scene, Desdemona enters with her kinsman Lodovico, an envoy from Venice. Since the Turkish threat is past, Othello is to be posted elsewhere, leaving Cassio as deputy in Cyprus. Othello is polite to the Venetians but offensive to Desdemona, even striking her in public to everyone's amazement. The Venetians begin to change their opinion of Othello. Is he going mad? Iago confirms their worst suspicions that 'he is much changed' (4.1.271).

Key quotes

Othello: A horn'd man's a monster and a beast.

(4.1.63)

Lodovico: Is this the noble Moor, whom our full senate
Call all-in-all sufficient? Is this the nature
Whom passion could not shake? Whose solid virtue
The shot of accident nor dart of chance
Could neither graze nor pierce?

Iago: He is much changed.

(4.1.266–270)

Key points

Iago's success is Othello's downfall; Othello incited to fury is now hellbent on Desdemona's murder. This scene of great dramatic intensity is a turning point for all – Desdemona, Othello, Iago and Cassio. Here Iago's Machiavellian cunning is truly evident and Othello's attempt to resist falters and fails in the absence of support or advice from anyone other than his own persecutor. The power of the scene lies in the characters and their interactions; tragedy now seems inevitable.

Scene 2

Summary: *Othello confronts Desdemona with charges of 'whore' but refuses to let her defend herself. Desdemona's innocence is evident and her love for Othello reaffirmed.*

Othello visits his wife, speaking first to Emilia at the door as though she were a brothel-keeper (thus revealing that he has already cast Desdemona as a prostitute, waiting inside the room for him, her 'customer'). At the end of a conversation she only half-understands, Othello accuses Desdemona of being a *'cunning whore of Venice'* (4.2.88). The women express their shock and disbelief to Iago, who assures them it's all a temporary 'humour' of Othello's. The scene ends with Iago inciting Roderigo to murder Cassio that night.

Key quote

Desdemona: His unkindness may defeat my life,
But never taint my love. I cannot say 'whore':
It does abhor me now I speak the word.

(4.2.158–161)

Key points

Othello's attitude to Desdemona and his treatment of her contrast strongly with his love for her at the end of 1.3.

Iago reassures Desdemona and Emilia that 'all things shall be well', but immediately after this begins persuading Roderigo (who complains that Iago has ill-advised him in his pursuit of Desdemona) that he should 'remove' Cassio in order to succeed with Desdemona.

While Desdemona's sadness and powerlessness in the situation are evident, she nobly reaffirms the strength of her love for Othello.

Scene 3 – The 'willow' scene

Summary: *As an introduction to the main scene, Othello orders Desdemona to go to bed, while he concludes a conversation with Lodovico. After the men have left, there follows a key scene for Desdemona and Emilia, known as 'the willow scene'.*

The 'willow' scene is named after the song that Desdemona's mother's maid, Barbary, sang after her lover who went mad forsook her. As Desdemona undresses, she sings a song about unfortunate love, and then the women talk intimately about men and relationships.

Key quotes

Desdemona: She had a song of willow;
An old thing 'twas; but it expressed her fortune,
And she died singing it.

(4.3.27–30)

Emilia:	... who would not make her husband a cuckold, to make him a monarch? ...
Desdemona:	Beshrew me, if I would do such a wrong ...
	(4.3.74–77)

Key points

Follow the conversation carefully. Do you share any of Emilia's views? Or Desdemona's? This scene contains key information to discuss issues of sexuality and the women's contrasting views of behaviour in relationships.

Othello appears to have regained his self-composure but there is an ominous tone in his order, 'Get you to bed on th'instant' (4.3.7). The contrast here between Emilia and Desdemona serves to highlight Desdemona's innocence and make more heinous Othello's murder of her. Her words to Emilia, 'If I do die before thee, prithee shroud me / In one of those same sheets (4.3.24–25) suggest her foreknowledge of her fate. Soon after this the sadness in her soul (or heart) is expressed in the willow song which not only prefigures her death but also expresses grief for the loss of her husband and his love of her – something she knows intuitively but cannot fathom.

Act 5

Scene 1

Summary: *Roderigo, reluctant, but yielding to Iago's pressures, 'kills' Cassio then is stabbed by Iago. Lodovico and Gratiano's arrival in response to cries for help almost undo Iago's schemes.*

Iago sets up Roderigo in the dark street to ambush Cassio: Othello, on his way to kill Desdemona, hears Cassio cry out but does not stay long enough to realise that Roderigo has only succeeded in wounding Cassio and is himself badly hurt. The fight attracts public attention. Sensing his plot unravelling, Iago stabs Roderigo, justifying the violence against Cassio's 'attacker'. He pointedly blames Bianca for causing the trouble and orders Emilia to run and tell Othello and Desdemona what has happened.

Key quote

Othello: ... O brave Iago, honest and just,
That hast such noble sense of thy friend's wrong,
Thou teachest me!

(5.1.31–33)

Key point

Treachery is most evident here in Iago's cold, scheming intelligence.

Scene 2

Summary: *Othello smothers Desdemona; Iago stabs Emilia; Othello gradually realises the extent of Iago's treachery and his dreadful mistake and stabs himself; Iago is condemned to death by torture.*

Othello hovers around the sleeping Desdemona. Notice how the pace of the scene quickens after she wakes at line 23. Realising how deluded Othello is, Desdemona tries to argue but knows she is certainly facing death at his hands. Othello smothers Desdemona but is disturbed by Emilia's arrival. Desdemona, on the point of death, cries out.

As the Venetians enter, Emilia knows it is Iago who engineered the lies and rumours. When she reveals the truth about the handkerchief, Iago stabs her to death. The wounded Cassio is carried in to testify and Othello, at last realising the extent of Iago's villainy, knows himself to be a fool and a murderer. After passing judgement on himself, Othello executes justice on himself in public. Iago is condemned to be tortured to death. Lodovico concludes the play by drawing Iago's attention to his handiwork, 'the tragic loading of this bed' (5.2.359).

Key quotes

Look closely at Othello's opening speech with its repeated use of light and references to Desdemona's purity.

Othello: Yet I'll not shed her blood,
Nor scar that whiter skin of hers than snow,
And smooth as monumental alabaster:
She must die, else she'll betray more men.

(5.2.3–6)

Desdemona: And you have mercy too. I never did
Offend you in my life; never loved Cassio
But with such general warranty of heaven
As I might love. I never gave him token.

(5.2.57–60)

Key points

Notice Othello and Emilia's wonderful use of language here as opposites collide poetically to work out the horrible truth of the situation (5.2.126–136). The truth dawns on Emilia at the end of this sequence as she repeats *'My husband!'* The word 'husband' is reiterated ten times in all, driving home Emilia's moment of realisation.

As the Venetians enter, Emilia knows it is Iago who engineered the lies and rumours. As she reveals the truth about the handkerchief, Iago stabs her to death. The wounded Cassio is carried in to testify and Othello, at last realising the extent of Iago's villainy, knows himself to be a fool and a murderer. After passing judgement on himself, Othello stabs himself in public. Iago is condemned to be tortured to death. Lodovico concludes the play by drawing Iago's attention to his handiwork, *'the tragic loading of this bed'* (5.2.359).

Watch the final scene in the Oliver Parker film version (1995): notice how the bed and all it symbolises becomes the final meeting place for the main characters in death.

Tragedy: The tragedy lies in the innocent and needless deaths that Iago's villainy and Othello's trust in the villain have caused. Othello sees the truth too late – by trusting Iago too well, he has rendered himself foolish and become a murderer who does not deserve to live. The deaths cause us to reflect on human destiny: 'Who can control his fate?' (5.2.263).

Justice: Discovery of Iago's true role in the tragedy leads to some form of just punishment. Do you think this suggests or restores a moral order in the world despite the havoc wreaked?

CHARACTERS & RELATIONSHIPS

Characters make the play come alive. What characters say and do and what happens to them not only tells the story literally but, more significantly, gives the readers of the text on the page and viewers of the scene in performance a multitude of thoughts about underlying themes and issues the play is dealing with.

For each character or relationship point noted below, I have indicated the scene (numbered in parentheses) where you should look for more detailed information to develop ideas.

Othello

You can trace a number of contrasts in Othello's fascinating tragic personality developed throughout the play. He is both a man of action and a fine speaker. Society honours him but his exotic background both attracts and disturbs the Venetians. He is a man of great calmness and leadership but also passionate, both sophisticated in some respects and fatally naive in others. These contradictions reveal a whole personality that is seen to be destroyed by Iago's malice working in combination with his own lack of judgement about others and anxiety about himself.

We learn quickly that 'the valiant Moor' is a respected soldier and proven defender of the Venetian state, which has honoured him (1.3). Montano and the gentlemen of the garrison waiting anxiously in Cyprus further confirm Othello's masterly soldiership (2.1) and it is clear that he is respected and well known to the islanders, who are happy to welcome him as Governor (2.2).

Outsider

Despite being recognised and welcomed by all, Othello is, paradoxically, clearly an outsider to the Italian community. His race sets him apart both physically, through his black skin, and culturally, as a foreigner with an exotic background and personal history. Certainly, Othello has been honoured and was welcomed at home by the Venetian Senator, Brabantio, until he overstepped Brabantio's unspoken social and racial tolerance boundaries by becoming the Senator's son-in-law (1.3).

First impressions of Othello

Our first impressions of Othello come from three characters who describe him as repulsive. Iago opens the play with strongly negative descriptions of Othello's bombastic style of speaking and arrogance in choosing his own officer. After Iago has shouted out gross sexual descriptions of Othello and Desdemona to Brabantio, Roderigo takes over to emphasise the usurper Othello's alien nature, describing him as an 'extravagant and wheeling stranger/ Of here and everywhere' (1.1.138–139).

Unable to figure out how Desdemona could have been attracted to such a fearful 'sooty bosom', Brabantio accuses Othello of witchcraft (1.2) before the assembled Senate of Venice.

Positive qualities

Our first sense of Othello's strong positive qualities, notably his dignified calmness at Brabantio's fuss over his marriage, comes from the man himself. He is not someone to be dictated to, confident in his own 'parts ... title, and ... perfect soul' (1.2). This masterful calmness is evident again when Othello arrives to sort out the night brawl in Cyprus (2.3).

At first, we see a sensible ruler, asking questions, approaching a disturbance logically. We admire his concern for the ordinary people of the island: he knows that 'civil disorder' and alarm bells ringing in the middle of the night will terrify people, whose 'hearts' are already 'brimful of fear'. It is this very habit of controlled passion, 'solid virtue', that Lodovico alludes to later in the play as being the noble Moor's outstanding characteristic, 'the nature/ Whom passion could not shake' (4.1.267).

Othello's frustration, impatience and rising passion

Othello's calm turns to angry passion through frustration in 2.3, as he attempts to extract a straight answer out of the roughed up and injured bunch of young men who are supposed to be a disciplined 'guard of safety' (2.3).

We monitor Othello's rising passion in the play through the way he uses language at different stages. In the Senate, he defends himself against the charge of witchcraft eloquently even though he protests (in a sort of rhetorical aside) that he is 'rude in speech' and will tell only a 'round unvarnished tale' (1.3). Surely he calculates the effect of telling such extraordinary travel stories to the sober Senators?

Significance of Othello's language patterns

Othello's elaborate language, particularly his habit of overstatement about his love for Desdemona, hints at a dangerously 'larger-than-life' view of life itself and the marriage relationship, which is one of complete dependence on his part. The calm measured language of the competent leader vies throughout the play with a more passionate (and poetic) emotion-laden expression. When he arrives in Cyprus, for example, he speaks of 'absolute content', adding the emotional flourish – with innocent prophetic irony – that 'if it were now to die / 'Twere now to be most happy' (2.1). More disturbing is the linking of 'love' and 'chaos' as a kind of parting compliment to Desdemona: 'And when I love thee not,/ Chaos is come again' (3.3). Even at the end, Othello overstates his love error as an excess, describing himself as 'one that loved not wisely, but too well' (5.2). It sounds sad and beautiful, but is it true, think you?

Because Othello is so characteristically in love with language, he is revealed to be especially susceptible to the effect of words spoken by others, and chiefly vulnerable to Iago's linguistic games, those repetitions, hesitations, slight inflexions and nuances demonstrated fully at work in 3.3 and 4.1.

As a single example of Othello's alternating language patterns, look at the scene containing his famous speech beginning 'Farewell the tranquil mind' (3.3.342–354). This is a beautiful but 'excessive' expression of passion that accepts Iago's insinuations about Desdemona and Cassio. He is still struggling to hold on to logic when he reverts to the language of enquiry (his 'commander' voice) by reasonably demanding 'ocular proof'. He then spins off again into linguistic excess with his 'Like to the Pontic sea' speech (3.3.450–459), the overblown rhetoric of which Iago cynically mocks by matching in his own vow that ends the scene.

Othello's sexuality

The issue of Othello's sexuality as a character trait is worth developing. As an older man, let alone a foreigner, other characters in the play ask whether he is fitting partner for Desdemona. He himself argues that he wants Desdemona with him as a companionable partner in Cyprus rather than simply to satisfy 'the palate of [his] appetite', meaning overwhelming sexual desire or 'heat' appropriate to young people, which he claims is 'defunct' in him (1.3.260–1). For more thoughts, see character notes on **Othello and Desdemona** and **Desdemona** below.

Othello may consider that his sexuality is under control but another aspect of his character, his apparent naivety about women, leaves him dangerously susceptible to Iago's attack. Iago can volunteer information about Venetian women's sly habits without fear of contradiction (3.3.200). More serious, because it leads Othello to speculate anxiously about his obvious racial difference as a 'problem', is Iago's suggestion that links sexuality with race. Desdemona, Iago hints, was excited by Othello's 'looks', and pretended to be afraid of him when she was really feeling desire (3.3.205). However spurious we consider the villain Iago's racist connection, Othello soon picks it up as something to ponder on, Desdemona's 'nature erring from itself' (3.3.225).

It isn't disparity of age that Iago targets directly, then, but the 'unnaturalness' of the interracial marriage (a racist attitude, by the way, and nothing to do with what might or might not be defined as 'natural'). This is a proposition Othello is very quick to accept, agreeing with the implicit slur both to himself as a black man and to Desdemona, a white woman whose genuine love choice has been negatively represented as an indicator of her 'thoughts unnatural' (3.3.231).

In an important soliloquy (3.3.255–274) Othello reveals his deepest fears about being thought 'old', 'black' and lacking conversation(!). Despite being undermined at once by Iago's insinuations, he tries to balance the paradox, still hanging on to shreds of belief in Desdemona's goodness and his own status. Notice how his slightly arrogant statement about the suffering of 'great ones' clearly includes himself – he casts himself as the 'tragic hero' if there is going to be a tragedy.

Appropriately for him, the sexual and poetic aspects of his love for Desdemona are restored in the tragic conclusion on their marriage and death bed. Othello's words about kissing and killing would have had a fitting, gently erotic *double entendre* for Shakespeare's audience (5.2.354–5). Elizabethan poetry is full of references to the lover's desire for 'death' (sexual orgasm), to be 'killed' in the arms of his beloved. The tragedy for Othello is that he finally regains certainty about his love through dying.

Q Do you think that Othello becomes the tragic hero that he himself suggested early in the play?

Iago

The riddle of Iago's character

Although this character is usually played by a senior actor onstage, the character tells Roderigo in conversation that his age is twenty-eight – he's still a young man with ambition (1.3.308). Iago has given rise to much critical speculation over the years about his motives. In the play, he himself offers several plausible reasons why he might want get even with Othello (sexual jealousy or disappointment at being passed over for promotion) and Cassio (jealousy and envy), although the riddle is actually insoluble – which is what makes the character so dramatically fascinating.

Interpretations of Iago

A nineteenth-century reader of the play considered Iago's malignity to be 'motiveless' – its very devilishness was what made it terrifying. A recent film version (Parker 1995) has read Iago's character as homoerotic, where an unresolvable desire for Othello leads him to destroy those who are closer than he is allowed to be. Another modern reading (the BBC version) has made Iago into a vicious NCO [non-commissioned officer, a junior rank in the army] spoiler, using his minor position of authority to get the better of his betters.

Different roles for different situations

My reading of Iago's character allows for any of these possibilities because he himself informs us that he delights in assuming different roles for different situations, like the older theatrical character of the 'Vice' (the comic villain) Shakespeare would certainly know and on whom he is clearly based. In the first scene of the play, Iago warns Roderigo (the foolish gentleman who is keeping Iago in cash) not to trust appearances, even revealing his own duplicity in the speech 'I am not what I am' (1.1.59–66).

He may enjoy playing the chameleon but we need to recognise that, through Iago's cruel manipulation, nobody in the play ends up being what he or she 'is' at the outset either. He happily fabricates false character sketches of Cassio to Montano (2.3) and of Othello to Lodovico (4.1) to serve his immediate purpose, while encouraging his victims to absorb messages about themselves and others, on trust, that then confuse or alter fundamental perceptions about reality.

Vicious as he is, Iago is also a supreme 'performer', completely aware of what is going on around him on the stage of fools, where he can simultaneously be involved as an actor and stage-manager. We hear his obviously theatrical voice enthusiastically taking over from Roderigo's feeble 'What, ho, Brabantio!' in 1.1, for example. Later, he performs to match Othello's rising passions, delirious with pleasure as he speaks ironically in answer to Othello's hope that he is 'honest' (3.3.371–7) and a moment later when mimicking Cassio talking in his sleep (3.3.410–23). His real *coup* is to stage-manage the conversation with Cassio about Bianca, which Othello mishears by Iago's design (4.1).

Is Iago psychopathic?

The wicked but entertaining Vice was the figure who traditionally drew out other characters to reveal faults in order to demonstrate a moral point. Iago's purpose, if he has one, goes much further than this because Shakespeare's play has developed characterisation far beyond two-dimensional moralising. Iago could be seen as psychopathic, that is (according to the Macquarie Dictionary), having 'a personality outwardly normal but characterised by a diminished sense of social responsibility, inability to establish deep human relationships, and sometimes, abnormal or dangerous acts'.

Under cover of darkness, Iago first reveals his corrupted imagination in the gross sexual imagery he thinks up to describe Othello and Desdemona as a sexual couple to Brabantio (1.1). Somehow he has convinced the people who matter that he is 'honest' (notice how many times that epithet is repeated in the play) – and he challenges the audience to refute it in his triumphant soliloquy (2.3), which goes on to exhibit the pointless cruelty of his plan to ensnare Othello, Cassio and Desdemona in the net of her own 'virtues'. This 'Divinity of hell!'

soliloquy identifies Iago as a self-styled devil who despises genuine honesty as mere weakness of will.

He is supremely scornful of virtue, another weakness, arguing to Roderigo that bodies are just like gardens to be used – we choose to plant what we like in them. 'Tis in ourselves that we are thus and thus' (1.3). The will, he argues, must control lust – then everything is possible.

This is the old Vice recast as genuine psychopath. He notices, as dawn breaks, how all the damage he's done in his first night on Cyprus (which he calls 'pleasure and action'), has made the time simply fly by (2.3). Later, his enjoyment of the argument between Othello and Desdemona in 3.4 is clear, especially when he appears to be solicitous but makes things worse for Desdemona to bear, by claiming to have seen Othello in the most stressful battle situation still able to keep his temper.

Some things can, nevertheless, get under Iago's skin. He counsels Roderigo to forget emotion and train the will, instead, which gives a person control over life and power over weaker wills (1.3) – yet he can be needled to express envy, jealousy and a sense of inferiority. His hatred of Cassio is partly grounded in an emotional response towards a rival who 'hath a daily beauty in his life/ That makes [Iago] ugly' (5.1).

Does Iago really suspect that Othello, and Cassio, have had sex with Emilia? Does he really think that Desdemona and Cassio could ever be lovers, given their personalities? Does he really lust after Desdemona himself (2.1.277–303)? He may have hit on one truth – that Cassio really does loves Desdemona – among all his nasty surmises.

A paradoxical trait

You should notice that Iago has one paradoxical trait in relation to women. Although he is seen to be a misogynist in his conversation with Emilia and Desdemona (2.1) his patience can be 'galled' by men paying attention to women, as when Cassio takes a kiss from his wife Emilia and then makes courtly gestures of finger-kissing with Desdemona (2.1). Iago's sexual thoughts seem to be expressed mostly in crude descriptive language, as we have seen. Look at the Parker film (1995) to see how the character has been imagined with his wife, using Emilia's body in a manner that is closer to rape than lovemaking.

Iago's use of words

Cassio, especially, irritates Iago by drawing attention more than once to Iago's lack of scholarship and breeding, moments of upper-class scorn which Iago stores up. Iago may not regard himself as an eloquent man – and he seems to envy Othello's ability to spin a tale – but he can use words tellingly to bait his victims, and that is ultimately all the skill he needs. In the last scene, Iago pointedly refuses to explain his actions against Othello, simply saying enigmatically 'what you know, you know' (5.2.300). His meaning gets through to Othello, who finally acknowledges his own faults and then executes himself while Iago watches in (satisfied?) silence.

Othello and Iago

In performance every construction of meaning follows from the way Othello and Iago are matched as actors and balanced as characters. Look at several productions on video, selecting key scenes like 3.3 and 4.1, and pay attention to the *mise en scène* (especially spatial dynamics) in which the two characters interact. Iago may be pushing emotional buttons but Othello's reactions have to be carefully judged, too. A strongly characterised Iago may help to check any tendency to overplay Othello as an egomaniac.

Iago pretends to respect Othello but reveals a racist mindset beneath what sounds initially like envy and disappointed ambition. He refers to 'the Moor, his Moorship' (1.1), characterising Othello's rich bossy talk as being full of 'bombast'. He tells Roderigo sneeringly that Desdemona loved Othello 'but for bragging and telling her fantastical lies' (2.1).

The relationship between Iago and Othello is therefore unequal from the start, with resentment on Iago's part. He quickly manoeuvres himself into a position of trust where he can exploit apparently loyal service to Othello for his own purposes. Despite wanting to bring Othello down, Iago continues to be the Moor's best character-reference for an audience: we believe he is speaking candidly when he says he knows that Othello is a good leader – 'another of his fathom they [the Venetians] have none' (1.1) – or acknowledges that Othello 'is of a free and open nature' (1.3) and 'is of a constant, loving, noble nature' and likely to be a good husband to Desdemona (2.1).

Othello's trust in Iago

Othello's belief in Iago's honesty is undiminished until the last moments of the play. This is largely why he never thinks to pursue issues of the deepest significance in conversation with anyone else. Iago, the 'man of honesty and trust', and his wife Emilia are Othello's first choice to look after Desdemona (1.3). He turns to 'honest Iago' to explain Cassio's part in the brawl when nobody else will give him a straight answer (2.3) and also trusts that Iago is telling the truth about sly Venetian women, which Iago reinforces by reminding him that his wife, Desdemona, is demonstrably a proven deceiver (3.3). Because Othello's 'occupation', or entire way of life that he knows, is to be a soldier, he is especially vulnerable to uncertainty after he has allowed his life to be compromised somewhat by getting married. Iago recognises in Othello's almost complete ignorance of 'social life' the weak spot in an otherwise strong marriage relationship – he triumphs when he brings Othello to the point of asking 'Why did I marry?' (3.3).

There are two hugely important scenes you must know well to really understand how Othello and Iago connect in this play: 3.3 and 4.1.

Act 3 Scene 3

In this scene, Iago nudges Othello verbally into taking notice of the possible significance of Cassio's conversation with Desdemona. She then begins her nagging campaign, which Othello at first good-naturedly allows. Seeing this encourages Iago to work harder after Desdemona leaves to make Othello genuinely suspicious. He does it by undermining Othello's faith in Desdemona's goodness, urging him to think of her as a woman who has done something 'against nature' by loving him. The scene ends with Othello admitting that Iago has set him 'on the rack', matched by an artificially 'passionate' outburst from Iago about the danger of being honest, 'Oh grace!' (3.3.371–378).

Act 4 Scene 1

The other scene is 4.1. Iago again tortures Othello with words and meanings to the point of inducing an epileptic seizure in his victim. He skilfully turns Othello's last remnants of pity to thoughts of murder by solicitously refuting Desdemona's virtues each time Othello recalls them.

Desdemona

We first see and hear Desdemona in the company of the senior men of her community, standing alone to defend her marriage choice before the Venetian Senate. She is respectful but not intimidated, sharing Othello's gift of eloquence while answering charges as both Brabantio's daughter and Othello's wife. Desdemona's strength impresses itself on the audience in that she establishes a sense of proportion and rightness in her actions. She boldly acknowledges her love and, when she realises that Othello has to leave for Cyprus immediately, she's adamant that she won't wait in Venice and certainly won't go back to her father's house (1.3).

Interpretations of Desdemona

Especially since the Victorian period, Desdemona has often been played as an innocent romantic, in love with Othello's exotic being, somewhat tepid as a personality onstage and doomed for a tragic end as her name suggests (Desdemona translates as 'unfortunate', or as Othello says finally, 'ill-starred'). While she is certainly idealised as a noble lady by the courtier Cassio, Desdemona has dramatic strengths which need to be embodied in performance. Othello knows that she is a brave and capable partner for him when he calls her his 'fair warrior' (2.1). She must be allowed to establish herself as chaste but worldly wise, in that she understands what Iago's rude jokes about women (2.1) and Emilia's frank truths about sex and men (4.3) mean, even if she doesn't endorse those views herself.

Desdemona's strengths

Desdemona rejoices in the very life and love Iago wants to crush or make sordid. Her good nature, strong spirits, positive attitudes and unshakeable values are revealed in every scene. For example, while she waits for Othello at Cyprus she politely joins in the conversation to mask her real anxiety about her husband still at sea (2.1). Once again, Iago characterises her accurately in conversation with Cassio as having 'so free, so kind, so apt, so blessed a disposition' (2.3). She will always do more than she's asked to do on someone else's behalf: her very virtues are what Iago knows will bring her down.

The short exchange with the clown (3.4) which is often omitted in performance actually illustrates very neatly Desdemona's capacity for wit. It catches a little moment of triumph as she thinks she's succeeded in winning Othello back to Cassio. The temporary anxiety of losing her handkerchief gives way to a gentle playfulness with Othello in the next brief conversation that turns unexpectedly sour. Even then, Desdemona blames herself for not being more aware of the demands of Othello's professional life, to which she attributes the bad temper.

Is Desdemona a deceiver?

Yes, in that she deceived her father, certainly (1.1). Her mask of light-heartedness in 2.2, noted above, is also 'false'. But we need to make a distinction about kinds of falseness that Othello never can make and Iago won't spell out. Sometimes, productions introduce an edge of uncertainty by letting her flirt with Cassio. In the play she justifies her friendliness to Cassio simply because he's a close friend of Othello's – to her mind, she is indirectly pleasing Othello (3.3). She takes up Cassio's anxious wish to stay in Othello's memory by insisting she'll be his friend: 'If I do vow a friendship I'll perform it/ To the last article' she says, just as Iago has predicted about her character (2.3).

Although modern playgoers may miss the connotation, an audience in Shakespeare's time would certainly have registered an ambiguous meaning in Desdemona's choice of words to Cassio. When she speaks of 'friendship' we know that she intends the term to be understood honourably, yet there was a sexual connotation in Shakespeare that could suggest a love affair. It still persists in contemporary speech in the phrase 'we are just good friends' that celebrities having affairs say to prying interviewers.

In this world of men, Desdemona the Venetian woman has to mind her language. Her unusual marriage against her father's wishes inevitably marks her as potentially troublesome. It is beyond Brabantio's wit to understand how a girl who has seemed to conform to standards of maidenly propriety so absolutely has taken it into her head to escape his controls. 'How got she out?' he asks, as though she is the family pet in heat and on the loose (1.1.170). We discover that she has not been interested in any local youth. This is not surprising if Roderigo – admittedly not the pick of the crop – is representative of the rich foppish type likely to make a marriage bargain with Brabantio.

How Desdemona's love for Othello is a trap

The tragic circumstance that traps Desdemona is that her love for Othello, the result of her free choice, becomes a fixed idea denoting her very deceptiveness in Othello's distorted thinking. She's condemned as an unnatural woman for choosing him in the first place, and further damned if she decides to change her mind again and 'repent', according to Iago's cruel argument (3.3).

We shouldn't underestimate her shock at Othello's physical violence in 4.1. She then endures further disgrace through Othello's accusation that she is a 'cunning whore of Venice' (4.2). This breakdown in the relationship develops naturally into Desdemona's 'swan song' in the Willow scene (4.3). She asks Emilia to make her bed with the wedding sheets (4.2) perhaps envisaging how Othello's violence may culminate in her death. Or she may be hoping to make a reconciliation between them by reminding him of their short time of happiness after the wedding.

Othello and Desdemona

As we have already seen, the marriage between Othello and Desdemona is susceptible to attack by its very unusualness and a certain ignorance of the partner on both sides. The courtship was built on a mixture of fascination, pity, exotic stories and kindness. Iago points out to Roderigo what could go wrong with the partnership in crude terms, when he argues that 'These Moors are changeable in their wills' and 'she must change for youth' (1.3) but, in fact, neither speculation is likely to occur and he knows it. Nevertheless, Iago is incapable of valuing their marriage as Othello and Desdemona obviously do, even if his description of it as a 'frail vow' between an 'erring barbarian' and a 'super-subtle Venetian' is made up for Roderigo's ears (1.3).

Their relationship begins as a tempered, mature passion on both sides, downplaying the sexual but not denying it altogether. Desdemona tells how she looks beyond the surface to see 'Othello's visage in his mind' (1.3.249). I don't think this should necessarily be read as meaning that she needed to look beyond Othello's surface appearance because the surface was unpleasing – there is never a hint of a suggestion that Desdemona holds racist ideas about her black husband. What she chooses to stress is his honour and 'valiant parts' (1.3) – but she's also determined to be beside his body as well as with his noble mind. She is going to be a dedicated wife to a professional soldier. Only after Othello has been poisoned by Iago does he become obsessed by sexuality as the basis for relationship. Like Desdemona, he is seen as an affectionate partner when the couple meet in Cyprus. Even Iago notices how 'well tuned' they are, vowing to make discord out of their harmony (2.1.293).

Desdemona tries to enter Othello's world of action, declining to be a 'moth of peace' (1.3.253), and he welcomes her desire to be part of that world because her presence enriches its significance for him. When she does participate in 'men's business', as a favour to Cassio, she mixes personal life with issues of state in a situation that is actually already out of her control (but firmly in Iago's hands). Every time she thinks she is doing Othello a favour by pleading for his friend Cassio she is harming her own relationship. Look at 3.4, where Othello demands the handkerchief while she insists on repeating Cassio's name, unaware of how Othello has been primed by Iago. Look then at 4.1, where, in conversation with the Venetian lords, her innocent comments about trying to help Cassio incense Othello to the point that he strikes her in public.

Power of words

Remember that words have been the basis for their courtship. We see the attraction Othello's words still have for Desdemona when he tells her of the handkerchief's magical significance. Because she takes his words to heart, she is horrified that she's mislaid it (3.4). The relationship inevitably breaks down when Othello can no longer speak meaningfully to her. A later scene (4.2) is shocking because it sets up a confrontation between Desdemona and Othello in a room that Othello characterises as a brothel – inferring that Desdemona is the prostitute, and he her sexual customer. Desdemona is stunned that the relationship has deteriorated so rapidly and searches around for the 'ignorant sin' she must have committed for

Othello to treat her with such disrespect. When Othello leaves, it is Iago who enters to hear Desdemona's impassioned statement of unswerving love for her husband – just the right/wrong person to appreciate the depth of her confusion and dismay.

Q Explore Desdemona's attitude to Cassio carefully. Does the text suggest an innocent friendship?

Q In your view, why is Desdemona unable to persuade Othello of her loyalty and innocence?

Emilia

Emilia is a problem. She is a loyal servant to Desdemona, although by picking up the handkerchief (3.3) and then keeping quiet about where it is – even after witnessing the argument (3.4) between Desdemona and Othello – she is directly responsible for the tragic misunderstanding that leads to Desdemona's murder. Emilia accurately diagnoses jealousy in Othello's behaviour and tries to warn Desdemona, who simply dismisses such a thing, that it is a dangerous 'monster' (3.4). Othello speaks to her vulgarly as though she is a brothel-keeper in 4.2, which makes her suspect that a troublemaker has been at work spreading false rumours about Desdemona, the kind of scandal she herself has suffered.

Knowing that relationships are fraught with jealous misunderstanding, Emilia's loyalty to Desdemona is nonetheless in conflict with her own married loyalty to Iago. As an obedient wife, she filches the handkerchief to please her husband (3.3), but is badly treated by him. The unpleasant sense of a joyless marriage is apparent in Iago's sharp wit directed against her and women in general (2.1), and his churlish thanks when she gives him the handkerchief, regretting her generosity immediately (3.3).

Emilia is a sexually aware, unromantic, worldly wise character. Her important speech in the Willow scene (4.3) about husbands and wives perhaps ought to be directed at the listening audience, even though she seems to be talking intimately to the patient loving wife, Desdemona.

Q Do you think Emilia's main purpose in the play is to expose Iago's villainy?

Desdemona and Emilia

As with Othello and Iago, these two roles need to be balanced in performance, so that Desdemona's sweetness can be given some challenging energy and Emilia's plain-speaking can be countered by a kinder view of human relationship. In the intimate scenes between these women, Emilia recognises Desdemona's distress and registers the change in behaviour of Othello but seems unable to put two and two together. Iago's guilt seems to take her completely by surprise. Perhaps it is a case of cognitive dissonance: she simply cannot bring herself to believe that Iago, the man who is her husband, is the core evil. At the point of death, Emilia vindicates Desdemona by telling the story of the missing handkerchief, which in turn implicates Iago (5.2).

Cassio

While Cassio is not a fully developed character but rather a representative type of honourable man, he is presented in a more complex way than as a sketchy secondary hero with his own 'fatal flaw'. Like Othello, he is also an 'outsider' to Venice, being a Florentine with different manners and ideas. Iago, who is envious because Cassio has been promoted to Othello's lieutenant, sneers at him to Roderigo for being a 'Florentine', a 'great arithmetician' and a 'bookish theoric' – all theory, no practical skills as a soldier (1.1). Cassio, on the other hand, considers Iago to be as 'kind' and 'honest' as any Florentine back home (3.1).

Cassio's personality

Cassio's personality is revealed in 2.3 and gives rise to speculation about his possibly suppressed feelings of love for Desdemona – which Iago suspects. Othello leaves him in charge of the night's partying in Cyprus that will celebrate the wedding night. Having received his orders from Othello and seen the couple leaving for their bedroom, Cassio immediately turns to Iago to set the watch. Look carefully at the language – it is as though Cassio is momentarily unsure of himself. Iago makes the real decision about what is a sensible time for the watch to start – first the lads should be allowed a few drinks. And he manages, without much effort, to persuade Cassio to have several drinks, after making a few imaginative remarks about the kind of 'sport' Othello must be enjoying with Desdemona. Cassio answers Iago politely, refusing to join in the lascivious talk. Within minutes, he is drinking, singing and, finally, fighting in a brawl where he inflicts serious injury on Montano. Cassio knows he shouldn't join in the Cyprus party with his men because he can't hold his liquor. Perhaps he is trying to drown his sorrows on Desdemona's wedding night, like Roderigo?

We wonder why Cassio seems surprised to hear that Othello is to be married (1.2). Can't he guess who the bride might be? Yet when he describes the marriage to Montano in Cyprus he's rapturous in praise of the 'divine Desdemona' and of the good marriage (note 2.1). Iago's eroticised reconstruction of Cassio's 'dream' (3.3) is interesting because it could have been stimulated by hearing Cassio talk in his sleep – though Iago's embroidery of details that suggest Cassio and Desdemona are lovers is no more than a daring invention.

How Cassio plays into Iago's hands

After the brawl, Cassio is ashamed of his behaviour, berating himself with a list of words to describe faults he has committed – slight, drunken, indiscreet, squabble, swagger, swear, wrath (2.3). Iago talks him round with 'come, you are too severe a moraller', suggesting that he ask Desdemona to intercede on his behalf with Othello. Emilia then passes on news to Cassio that Othello is making an example of him for injuring Montano but will soon restore him, and that he has Desdemona's support (3.1). Cassio could leave it at that, but he doesn't – he asks to see Desdemona personally. This, again, is exactly what Iago needs – to bring Cassio and Desdemona together in Othello's sight. Being a gentleman, Cassio also arranges an *aubade* (3.1), some morning wake-up music traditionally played outside the bedchamber of newly-married couples. Given the disturbance of the night before, this is ill-judged and a poor omen to Cassio when Othello sends the clown to silence the musicians.

Cassio and Bianca

Bianca's interaction with Cassio shows another, less honourable, side to his nature – he wants her to do something for him but is reluctant to be seen in public with her because she is a prostitute (3.4). Her jealous outburst over the handkerchief is a minor reflection of, but equivalent to, Othello's. Cassio's disrespectful view of the courtesan Bianca as a sexual partner, expressed in 4.1, needs to be contrasted with his over-idealisation of Desdemona's virtues – especially as he seems to forget how much he's been pestering her to use her charms on Othello to get something for him.

Roderigo

Roderigo, Iago's 'purse' (source of money) and pawn, is usually played as a comic weakling but this may need to be discussed. Look carefully: he's rich, vicious, sly, and wants to have Desdemona sexually – is this love or lust? It is easy for Iago to motivate him to violence and it seems like no more than poetic justice that he ends up mortally wounded by the man he trusted to procure Desdemona for him. Roderigo's character has evolved out of an earlier folk-play tradition, where a cowardly comic suitor (bound to lose out) is set up against more suitable heroic rivals.

While Roderigo's weak character is sustained, make sure you understand his deeper purpose in the play – his importance to Iago's success and his role in Othello's tragedy.

Brabantio

Brabantio is important because he reflects racist attitudes and is a typically theatrical 'father' of the time, anxious to protect the daughter who is his investment in the marriage market. How easily he believes Iago's obscenities because they echo the anxiety dream he's been having. His anger at being deceived by his girl becomes a general warning to all fathers in the audience – 'trust not daughters' minds' (1.1). Brabantio is so sure of his importance that he feels able to attack Othello physically in the street, accusing him of witchcraft, and grumbling that, if Othello is allowed to get away with this, 'bondslaves and pagans' will be running the state before long (1.2).

In the Senate, Brabantio's begrudging acceptance of Othello introduces a dangerous warning to Othello about Desdemona's likely future deceptiveness. Look carefully at the way he mockingly refutes the

Duke's comforting platitudes (1.3.200–217). Once again in Shakespeare, a ruler is seen to be ineffectual in trying to patch up serious differences. Brabantio tells him that it's all very well to listen to comforting talk but you don't mend a broken heart with words.

THEMES, IDEAS & VALUES

Appearance and reality

This play raises many issues but they can all be seen to stem from a fundamental thematic concept – the relationship between appearance and reality in shaping human understanding and relationships. The play encourages us to think about how things look on the surface as opposed to the truth of the matter – which may be unacceptable, deliberately concealed or simply unknown as yet – reminding us to be aware how much we tend to rely on appearances and can be taken in by outward show or sly words.

This theme is common in Shakespeare's plays, as you may have realised already from the plays you know. In *Othello*, it is opened in many ways:

- Why can't Brabantio trust the outward behaviour of his daughter, for example?
- Iago pointedly advises Roderigo not to trust outward show.
- Desdemona argues that she saw Othello's mind in his visage, looking beyond surface to inner worth, beyond the 'sooty bosom' that so frightens Brabantio.

Act 1.3 begins by laying down this fundamental thematic as the Duke and his advisers guess, despite conflicting evidence, 'a pageant to keep us in false gaze', that the Turks are really heading for Cyprus. Good rulers think beyond appearance, what's on the surface, to the real issue.

These cool measured men are still capable of error, nonetheless, if they respond to the moment and speak before thinking of consequences. The Duke promises to punish whoever has done wrong to Brabantio, even if he is 'our proper son' (1.3), just as Othello later speaks before realising he's condemning his friend Cassio (2.3). The Duke, however, takes time to actually find out the truth by listening, while Othello makes his judgement after hearing only Iago's 'truth' which is necessarily false. Othello's jealousy, crucially, is fed by accepting appearances.

The following themes and issues may be developed further by referring back to this one fundamental thematic.

Love

The word 'love' and its meanings

The very word 'love', in whatever language, is likely to conjure up a complicated range of ideas, thoughts, feelings and associations for people worldwide. Western consumer society gets an annual reminder of the all-pervasive 'romantic' concept several weeks before 14 February in the shape of red roses, hearts, chocolates, and funny or sentimental Valentine's Day cards for sale.

Speaking again of Western culture, it isn't hard to notice signs of 'love' at a superficial level, expressed in the kind of entertainment we like to watch, advertising images. Our own everyday habits of conversation attribute many feelings, wishes and dreams to the word, such as 'I love pizza', 'don't you just love Robert Pattinson?', 'I love my pit bull terrier', 'I love windsurfing', 'love your hair colour', 'wouldn't you love to just get on an plane and go somewhere exciting ...'.

When it comes to talking seriously about 'love' as a deeply felt emotion for another person – perhaps someone you might want to have a relationship with – many people find it difficult to say what they mean. They might even wonder what the feeling is, anyway – how do you know when you love someone? Or when you are in love? Is 'being in love' the same as 'loving'? Is it the same as sex? Or just another word for a sexual relationship? And if you allow yourself to love somebody, you know that you are taking some big emotional risks. Will that person really be your heart's desire? Is trust a crucial component of love? What if you are rejected? What about the opinion of other people you care about? What happens when love has to accept changes in a financial crisis, or bad health, or danger? Culture and upbringing also help to determine how appropriate it is to express feelings of love in the first place. All these points are worth developing because they have a bearing on the way we are likely to read the tragic situation in *Othello*.

Love between couples in *Othello*

The love between Othello and Desdemona seems to be strong and founded on mutual respect and fascination with the other person, including but not dominated by sexual desire. What makes it change? Who changes? One of the issues, noted in the discussion of Othello's character, is naivety. Being made to feel inadequate or ignorant is a crippling experience for any person and can affect a relationship deeply. Conversely, the kind of worldly wisdom Iago and Emilia profess to have can lead to jaded or cynical views about the possibility of knowing love at all – or simply equating love with having sex, and sex with nothing more significant than a commodity for sale.

Q Discuss the love between Othello and Desdemona in more detail, taking into account the basis of their attraction and each character's attitudes and feelings as events change.

Q Does the play suggest that love is fickle or that 'true love' does not exist? Or do you think that *Othello* shows that love is a casualty of men's scheming and weaknesses?

Jealousy

Iago knows precisely how to undermine Othello's fragile experience of love when he introduces the idea of the 'green-eyed monster, which doth mock/ the meat it feeds on' (3.3). Jealousy does feed on the jealous person. If I am jealous, the person I feel jealous towards may have no inkling of the hostility I'm directing silently at him or her and so, of course, that makes my jealousy even more intense and bitter to bear. I lose sleep and feel churned up, the object of my jealousy appears to thrive. I feel jealous in the first place because I perceive that someone else has (or has taken) what I consider is rightfully mine. Jealousy is rooted in the fear that we may lose something or someone precious to us. Envy, by contrast, is the feeling we experience when someone legitimately has something, or some relationship, or a character trait, or some stroke of luck that we want or wish we had. Envy is terrible but jealousy is worse, perhaps.

Iago says he's jealous of Othello because there has been gossip about Othello and Emilia, his wife. He also claims to feels jealous of Cassio for getting the job he thinks he deserved and he also probably envies Cassio for being a gentleman with charm and privilege. Roderigo is jealous of Othello for winning Desdemona, the bride he wanted and thought he'd won through Iago's agency. Othello is made jealous of Cassio for stealing Desdemona, and Bianca is jealous of the woman who gave Cassio that handkerchief.

Jealousy is a phantom, as Emilia knows well enough when she says that 'jealous souls ... are not ever jealous for the cause,/But jealous for they're jealous' (3.4.155–8). There is no reason for any of the characters to believe that any of their jealous suppositions are true. But jealousy is always on the lookout for clues and doesn't need much evidence. It is even more likely to see what it fears if the subject is primed with lies: Othello only has to see Cassio laughing to assume he's discussing Desdemona, for instance (4.1). He only has to see Desdemona hesitate about the whereabouts of the handkerchief and keep insisting on Cassio's name to feel an upsurge of jealous rage (3.3).

Read psychiatrist Anthony Storr's essay 'Othello and the Psychology of Sexual Jealousy' (1989) for a fascinating discussion of the subject.

Trust

Trust is the most fundamental gift we have to give or receive – and can be exploited to give us trouble and pain. Betrayal, then, is a catastrophic negation of trust. It leads to the habit of cynicism (that sneering refusal to accept anything on trust because nobody is worth trusting) or a feeling of constant nervous suspicion. Trust is related to honesty and honour, it is about being honest in, or honouring, relationships with other human beings. *Othello*, therefore, explores the tragic outcome of quite reasonably putting trust in a person accounted by pretty well everybody to be 'honest'. Every lie that Iago tells goes unquestioned because he is known to be 'honest': the epithet is repeated throughout the play by every character he encounters and, most fundamentally, is how Othello habitually defends him for daring to 'speak up' in a difficult situation.

'The Moor is of a free and open nature' Iago knows, and so is Desdemona: they are therefore easy targets for his lies. Desdemona never ceases to trust Othello completely, just as Othello, the naive man in love, initially assumed she was trustworthy. Desdemona trusts Cassio's honour implicitly, too. Knowing he is both a gentleman and (because everything in the play suggests she is innocent of adultery) that he would never lie about her sexually, she defends him – even on her deathbed – against Othello's lie that he has 'used' her (5.2).

Emilia suspects that her trust in Iago is probably unwarranted and she certainly doesn't trust Othello, because of his unpredictable temper towards Desdemona. But Emilia herself is untrustworthy because she fails to tell Desdemona about the handkerchief, although she has more than one opportunity to explain why it's lost and who has it.

Roderigo, the 'gull'd gentleman' (a 'gull' being a fool who can be easily tricked) trusts Iago, even though Iago has told him not to trust outward appearance, and gets himself killed – by Iago. Cassio similarly trusts Iago, is easily made drunk, gets himself sacked, then gets Desdemona into trouble with her husband.

Women and relationships

Since Shakespeare's times things have certainly changed for women in Western society, in both public activities and in the management of personal relationships, yet visitors to Elizabethan and Jacobean England registered their astonishment and delight to see the comparatively 'free' lives of women citizens, in comparison with girls and women in Catholic Europe at that time. Nonetheless, well-born women anywhere, like Desdemona, would have lived supervised lives in their parents' home, under paternal control until the day they passed as virgins into the hands of their new husbands to breed legitimate heirs. Containment was deemed essential to ensure that girls remained unsullied – damaged goods were not easy to marry off.

Even so, debate about women's roles as sexual and life partners, with rights to speak and act, were being revalued and debated in pamphlets (some written by women, such as the pseudonymous 'Jane Anger'), plays like Shakespeare's own *Taming of the Shrew* and moral tracts circulated for public information or children's education. Emilia was not alone in expressing forthright views about men being as responsible as women for good behaviour all round (4.3), even though Desdemona's attitude of forbearance would still have been admired as a greater feminine virtue.

Consider how the three women in the play represent models of female behaviour in relation to men – and how men respond to them. How do they express themselves verbally and what degree of choice do they appear to have? I notice, for example, how Emilia, for all her boldness when she is alone with Desdemona, another woman, has to insist on being allowed to stay and speak when Iago orders her home (5.2). Notice how Cassio, the gentleman, may respect Desdemona as a goddess, feel it's his right to kiss another man's wife (Emilia) in friendly greeting in public, and deal with a doting prostitute (Bianca) quite roughly, openly making fun of her foolish aspiration to be his wife.

Racism

Racism is about several things at different levels of perception or misperception. It takes notice of outward signs, by which it judges the worth of the person: some of these signs are biological and physiological like skin colour (the prime indicator for the racist), body size and shape, vocal sound and so on, while others are the consequence of culturally learned differences seen in things like dress, food preferences, manners and habits. Deeper racist attitudes focus on maintaining a separation between the alien and the familiar (usually polarised as black and white), by insisting on tribal identification and mobilising fears of takeover, or loss of identity. Racist responses can be sparked by sexual anxiety or envy, religious or ethical conflicts – or nothing in particular except learned antipathy. Tensions are not always easy to locate, articulate or resolve.

It could be argued that racism and awareness of racist attitudes are elements of modern culture and ought not to be made into an issue for *Othello*, which was written and first performed before people were generally aware of what 'racism' meant. This is a naive argument, I think, considering that in Shakespeare's lifetime England was engaged in racial suppression of native elements in its 'own' territories (Scotland, Ireland and Wales), not to speak of aggressive colonising ventures in the New

World. In my reading of *Othello*, Brabantio and Iago are two overt racists, and there are suggestions of covert racism in the Duke, which suggests that it was a recognisable issue and of interest to Shakespeare.

You need to think about this point, also, because it affects the way the play is cast, performed and discussed nowadays. Othello is a North African Moor, a black man, and therefore an unusual but not completely unknown sight in Shakespeare's London, during a time of aggressive colonial expansion. Blackamoor characters occasionally appeared in early drama, although (like Aaron, the Moor in Shakespeare's bloodthirsty Roman tragedy *Titus Andronicus*) they were likely to be identifiably colour-coded villains.

The first actor to play Othello was probably Richard Burbage, Shakespeare's main performer, his face blacked with burnt cork. Until recently the plum role has been taken almost entirely by senior white performers, often aiming at creating the impression of a generic kind of black person. Chief among these is Laurence Olivier's reading of the character, where Othello is Jamaican (1965, available on film). In the BBC's 1994 version Anthony Hopkins re-creates the character of a Jacobean Moor.

So who is to play Othello and in what way? The American black actor, Hugh Quarshie, presented a lecture to the International Shakespeare Association in 1999 in which he talked about the difficulty of acting what he believes to be racist play nowadays, especially if you are a black actor – is it still a plum role? His argument is that a black actor playing Othello inevitably reinforces the racist inferences in the characterisation. (I'm not sure I fully agree with the argument Quarshie puts forward but it needs to be considered.) On the other hand, Janet Suzman, the South African actress and anti-apartheid supporter, has argued: 'Othello can no longer, I believe, be played by a white actor. It would be neither fitting nor dignified nor believable' (Suzman 1996, p.59).

Xenophobia – fearing the outsider

Othello may be black but he is also foreign to Venice and therefore an outsider in another way. To be identified as an 'outsider' by any group means that the protection offered by the group to its members cannot be counted on – or has been forfeited by the very virtue of being identified as 'other'.

Othello isn't the only outsider in the play. Cassio, an Italian but belonging to a rival city, Florence, is equally alien. Desdemona, too, positions herself as an outsider, both because she is a woman defying the established Venetian patriarchal authority and as a woman of a particular class and status who chooses a partner outside her permitted sphere. Roderigo is almost an outsider because he is ineffectual, on the periphery of gentility, and therefore only recognised by Brabantio as the lesser evil for a son-in-law when Othello is the alternative.

Reputation

'Reputation' nowadays is a term that is associated either with sexual exploits ('good', 'bad' or 'lost' reputation) or used as an affirmation of credibility or quality that deserves respect. In Shakespeare's time, reputation had a deeply serious meaning for a person in terms of a 'good name'. Associated with the masculine code of conduct, 'reputation' went beyond the regulation of one's personal behaviour to avoid public scandal. It indicated self-esteem tied up with the esteem of others, an ongoing public evaluation of one's worth. It was one of the princely virtues, indicative of leadership with moderation and fairness, inseparable from its companion ideal of 'honour'. Similarly for a woman, 'reputation' went beyond having a 'good name' for keeping herself sexually honourable and was related to a much greater ideal of 'virtue', a cluster of traits that attracted respect. Desdemona's reputation is never questioned even for making a marriage with Othello because she does not act to dishonour herself – she is seen as a virtuous wife. Brabantio is temporarily outraged but not publicly shamed by his daughter's act, therefore. Iago, too, does not target her reputation when he insinuates to her husband that her choice was 'unnatural'.

We still value and recognise the noble act even though the world in the early twenty-first century gives us more daily examples of corruption and self-interested behaviour than acts of genuine honour, worthy of a good 'reputation'. Cassio mourns for his lost 'reputation' as 'the immortal part of [him]self' (2.3). Othello, too, makes a last effort to salvage his 'reputation' when he asks to be understood as 'an honourable murderer', 'For naught did I in hate, but all in honour' (5.2. 291–2).

DIFFERENT INTERPRETATIONS

Different interpretations arise from different responses to a text. Over time, a text will give rise to a wide range of responses from its readers, who may come from various social or cultural groups and live in very different places and historical periods. These responses can be published in newspapers, journals and books by critics and reviewers, or they can be expressed in discussion among readers in the media, classrooms, book groups and so on. While there is no single correct reading or interpretation of a text, it is important to understand that an interpretation is more than a personal opinion – it is the justification of a point of view on the text. To present an interpretation of the text based on your point of view you must use a logical argument and support it with relevant evidence from the text.

Critical viewpoints

This play has had a long critical and performance history, surviving with some cuts but no major adaptations through the changing public tastes of Restoration England, (where, for the first time, women instead of boys played the female parts), and through the eighteenth century and Victorian periods, when serious dramatic criticism came into being.

The English neo-classical critic Thomas Rymer gave a famously negative assessment of the play in 1693 (See Alexander, 1968, for a full discussion). Objecting to Shakespeare's flouting of decorum, he described it as a 'bloody farce without salt or savour', specifically citing Othello and Desdemona's marriage as 'monstrous and improbable'. He also objected to Othello's high military rank in a white Christian society. Most subsequent critics have not challenged Rymer (who ignored evidence in Shakespeare's text which didn't agree with his preconceived opinions), although they all acknowledge the play has minor difficulties in the mismatched time schemes and major challenges in the interpretation of complex character behaviour.

Critics habitually point out that an audience usually fails to notice discrepancies in the time scheme because the action is so absorbing. Only when analysing the text do you realise that logically there must be long time gaps (unmentioned in the play) for people to travel over the sea and for messages between Venice and Cyprus to be exchanged. So, logically, there *could* be time for Iago's suggestion of infidelity to occur, time for Desdemona to get tired of old soldier Othello and be seduced by young Cassio.

Much more interesting in performance is the condensed time scheme of the psychological and emotional plot, driven by Iago's opportunistic scheming in Acts 2 and 3, that seems to progress in an unstoppable frenzied burst. The feeling is so intense that audiences aren't troubled by implausible anomalies in 'real' time. The whole point of the play is that Othello is misled and driven by emotional pain to murderous jealousy, Desdemona is unsuspecting, innocent and loyal, and Iago is a marriage-wrecker and soul-destroyer (Bullough 1973, 232). How and why Iago manages this and what others fail to perceive is the core of the play.

A.C. Bradley's major study (1904) is rather Victorian in tone but covers all areas of critical significance, especially in its meticulously detailed character portraits. Most subsequent critical approaches dealing with race and racism, gender or psychological issues tend to work from detailed character analysis. Othello, Desdemona and Iago continue to be the main focus of these studies. Leslie Fiedler's detailed chapter on *Othello* in *The Stranger in Shakespeare* (1974) discusses Othello as Moor and Desdemona as independent woman in detail, both as examples of 'outsiders'.

Coleridge's comment on Iago's apparently 'motiveless malignity' initiated an important line of critical enquiry about that character: Spivack (1958) argues that Iago is more like the Devil himself than a Vice figure. (See also Scragg 1968.) Iago's evil mind can also be approached from an historicist perspective, comparing Shakespeare's character with others in contemporary plays that reflect a Jacobean fashion for Machiavellian villains and cynics.

Other critical approaches deal with language structures, the historical and psychological geography of the text (e.g. Kernan, in the Snyder collection) and the play's predominant night setting and dark imagery (Holloway). The lost handkerchief, such a small but vital prop, attracts critical attention because of the thematic issues related to it: what provokes jealousy? How can proof, 'ocular' or otherwise, be tested and validated before taking violent action? What makes people susceptible to being fooled?

The indefinable but strangely symbiotic relationship between Othello and Iago explored by almost all critics has influenced stage and film realisations of the play. See the Olivier/Finlay, Hopkins/Hoskins and Fishburne/Branagh pairings. Actors occasionally alternate roles to explore this relationship further.

Two interpretations

Here are two different, but possible, readings of *Othello*.

Reading 1

Othello is both defined, yet ultimately undermined, by his occupation. One way to interpret Othello's susceptibility to Iago's lies is to compare what he understands with what he cannot know or find out. Othello's occupation is military – as a Moor in a Venetian Christian society, he's accepted because he's a successful general, respected for what he does rather than who he is. This is made clear in 1.3, where the Venetian state, in the person of the Duke, defends Othello publically. Othello immediately reinforces his civic position by insisting that his marriage will not deflect him from his military duty.

Once the Turkish threat is cancelled and Cyprus is under control, what is there for Othello to do? Paradoxically, he explains how he feels most 'content' on the battlefield because he understands what to do and can act decisively (3.3). When Iago mounts his cunning attack, Othello doesn't see it for what it is and has no defences ready.

When forced to think about the possibility of Desdemona's unfaithfulness, Othello looks to himself first to identify supposed deficiencies in his socially recognised persona. Perhaps it's because he's black or too old for her? He rejects these ideas but is worried that she might find him uncouth in comparison with gallant Cassio, because he 'lacks soft parts of conversation/ That chamberers have' (3.3). He rejects Cassio's *aubade* (3.1) perhaps because he's still concerned by the disturbances of the previous night but also, as the Clown says, because he's not pleased by this music. The sound he prefers is a combination of horses neighing, trumpets, drums, shrill fifes – the music of a battlefield. Once that is all silenced by peace and marriage, it is a sign that his 'occupation's gone', too (3.3).

Unlike the politically framed world of Shakespeare's other three mature tragedies, *Othello* is a tragedy about love, set in an urban domestic environment. Before Desdemona met him and he fell in love with her, there's no evidence in the play that Othello (the busy soldier who impressed Desdemona most with the hardness and danger of his life) has had much to do with women or domesticity. He lives in the homocentric world of comrades, surrounded by and relating to men he commands. Whether or not he consciously believes his own story about the magic power of his mother's handkerchief, when he frightens Desdemona it is certainly symptomatic of his growing anxieties about his own response to the state of his marriage (3.4). Sex and violence come together in his mind and have to be held in check by powerful charms: his clear implication is that, just as his mother subdued his father and made him into a docile husband, so Desdemona needs to treasure the same talisman to keep herself and Othello in harmony. His expressed belief that he loved 'not wisely but too well' articulates his own tragically true epitaph as the great soldier. Othello is conquered by a genuine love and perplexed to be in that vulnerable position without any military wisdom to comprehend or defend it.

Reading 2

The women display greater fortitude than the military men of *Othello*.

All three women in the play may be interpreted in ways that challenge conventional stereotypes. Is Desdemona a doomed victim from the outset (as her name suggests)? Is Emilia her foil, a jaded wife wise in the ways of the world? Is Bianca just a petulant clinging 'fitchew' (polecat, whore)? Shakespeare's text itself invites actors to challenge each of these stereotypes in performance to explore questions, which may not be answerable directly in the text, about the behaviour and deeper motivations of each woman.

Like Cordelia in *King Lear,* Desdemona is a brave adult daughter who inevitably defies her father's controlling masculinity by asserting a new husband's claim to her love (1.3). Iago seizes on this point, perverts it and returns it to a horrified Othello, making Desdemona's professed strength of love for her husband into a condemnation, proof of her capacity to deceive him just as she deceived her father. Why does Desdemona lie to Othello about the handkerchief when he demands to see it (3.4)? Why does she accuse herself of being her own killer just before she dies?

It is surely a mistake in interpretation to offer any hint that Desdemona is false to Othello – the whole point of the tragedy is that she is an active, intelligent and unsuspecting victim. In every way she is a worthy wife to Othello. The audience sees her dodging of Othello's question about the handkerchief as a natural, nervous response – she's worried about Othello's agitation but also genuinely wants to talk about Cassio (3.4). Look for mixed, complex motivations in scenes where she appears to be flirting verbally with Iago or showing interest in Lodovico (2.1, 4.3).

More difficult questions surround Emilia. She loves Desdemona and knows how much Desdemona values the handkerchief. Emilia has several opportunities to speak up about taking it, so why does she leave it so late (5.2)? Her relationship with Iago is demonstrably sour, yet she steals for him and cannot believe the depth of his malignity, which she has interpreted as jealous suspicion.

How can we interpret her forthright comments to Desdemona in 4.3? Is she, behind the worldly advice about using sex for advantage, simply trying to educate the guileless bride in the realities of adult relationships? Does an audience share any of Emilia's attitudes to Othello throughout the play? Iago's verbalised comments about women show him to be a misogynist (woman hater) – so what is the attraction to Emilia?

Bianca, the Cypriot courtesan, whose name suggests the 'whiteness' of chastity, is also to be interpreted as being more than she first appears. The way Cassio treats her and speaks disparagingly of her to Iago (in Othello's sight but not hearing, 4.1), reveals his less-than-courtly side, which he reserves solely for Desdemona. You might discern in this some ambiguity about his feelings for Desdemona, since he apparently lies to Iago (1.2) about guessing who Othello has married yet has reportedly been a familiar go-between for the lovers, according to Othello (3.3) – something for Iago to exploit.

Bianca's flare-up of jealousy about the handkerchief Cassio claims he 'found' in his lodgings (and honestly did so, we know), may be more motivated than Othello's, since she is clearly less secure of Cassio's mocking affection and his feelings may indeed place her in rivalry with Desdemona (3.4). Bianca's implication in Roderigo's murder by Iago (5.1) is completely unjustified, because it occurs before she appears on the scene and all her anxieties are obviously for Cassio, who 'supped at [her] house' and is now badly wounded. Iago plays on the other men's prejudices to divert suspicion from himself. Notice how Emilia (who we know has racy thoughts about men and sex) supports Iago by casting aspersions on Bianca and is very affronted when Bianca claims to live as 'honest' (sexually proper) a life as herself (5.1).

Each woman in the play demands a careful reading rather than a lazy application of a stereotype. Each one opens up questions of interpretation in relation to how men see or want to see women, and how the sexualised nature of female characters is one of the difficult driving forces in this love tragedy.

QUESTIONS & ANSWERS

This section focuses on your own analytical writing on the text and gives you strategies for producing high quality responses in your coursework and exam essays.

Essay writing – an overview

An essay is a formal and serious piece of writing that presents your point of view on the text, usually in response to a given essay topic. Your 'point of view' in an essay is your interpretation of the meaning of the text's language, structure, characters, situations and events, supported by detailed analysis of textual evidence.

Analyse – don't summarise

In your essays it is important to avoid simply summarising what happens in a text:

- A **summary** is a description or paraphrase (retelling in different words) of the characters and events. For example: 'Macbeth has a horrifying vision of a dagger dripping with blood before he goes to murder King Duncan'.
- An **analysis** is an explanation of the real meaning or significance that lies 'beneath' the text's words (or images in a film). For example: 'Macbeth's vision of a bloody dagger shows how deeply uneasy he is about the violent act he is contemplating – as well as his sense that supernatural forces are impelling him to act'.

A limited amount of summary is sometimes necessary to let your reader know which part of the text you wish to discuss. However, always keep this to a minimum and follow it immediately with your analysis (explanation) of what this part of the text is really telling us.

Plan your essay

Carefully plan your essay so that you have a clear idea of what you are going to say. A plan will ensure that your ideas flow logically, that your argument remains consistent and that you stay on the topic. An essay plan should be a list of **brief dot points** – no more than half a page. It includes:

- your central argument or main contention – a concise statement (usually in a single sentence) of your overall response to the topic. See 'Analysing a sample topic' for guidelines on how to formulate a main contention.
- three or four dot points for each paragraph indicating the main idea and evidence/examples from the text. Note that in your essay you will need to *expand* on these points and *analyse* the evidence.

Structure your essay

An essay is a complete, self-contained piece of writing. It has a clear beginning (the introduction), middle (several body paragraphs) and end (the last paragraph or conclusion). It should also have a central argument that runs throughout, linking each paragraph to form a coherent whole.

See examples of introductions and conclusions in the 'Analysing a sample topic' and 'Sample answer' sections.

The introduction establishes your overall response to the topic. It includes your main contention and outlines the main evidence you will refer to in the course of the essay. Write your introduction *after* you have done a plan and *before* you write the rest of the essay.

The body paragraphs argue your case – they present evidence from the text and explain how this evidence supports your argument. Each body paragraph needs:

- a strong **topic sentence** (usually the first sentence) that states the main point being made in the paragraph
- **evidence** from the text, including some brief quotations
- **analysis** of the textual evidence explaining its significance and **explanation** of how it supports your argument
- **links back to the topic** in one or more statements, usually towards the end of the paragraph.

Connect the body paragraphs so that your discussion flows smoothly. Use some linking words and phrases like 'similarly' and 'on the other hand', but don't start every paragraph like this. Another strategy is to use a significant word from the last sentence of one paragraph in the first sentence of the next.

Use key terms from the topic – or synonyms for them – throughout, so the relevance of your discussion to the topic is always clear.

The conclusion ties everything together and finishes the essay. It includes strong statements that emphasise your central argument and provide a clear response to the topic.

Avoid simply restating the points made earlier in the essay – this will end on a very flat note and imply that you have run out of ideas and vocabulary. The conclusion is meant to be a logical extension of what you have written, not just a repetition or summary of it. Writing an effective conclusion can be a challenge. Try using these tips:

- Start by linking back to the final sentence of the second-last paragraph – this helps your writing to 'flow', rather than just leaping back to your main contention straight away.
- Use synonyms and expressions with equivalent meanings to vary your vocabulary. This allows you to reinforce your line of argument without being repetitive.
- When planning your essay, think of one or two broad statements or observations about the text's wider meaning. These should be related to the topic and your overall argument. Keep them for the conclusion, since they will give you something 'new' to say but still follow logically from your discussion. The introduction will be focused on the topic, but the conclusion can present a wider view of the text.

Essay topics

1. Iago says: "The Moor is of a free and open nature". Does this explain why Iago is able to deceive Othello so easily?
2. 'Desdemona is no more than a passive victim of people who should care for her.' Do you agree?
3. 'Othello is much more a story of jealousy than of love.' Do you agree?
4. 'Othello suggests the foolishness of entering a relationship at odds with the surrounding society's standards.' Discuss.
5. To what extent does the issue of race determine Othello's downfall?
6. The play is called *Othello* but the villain Iago is the character we want to talk about most. Should we retitle the play *Iago*? Give your reasons for arguing either way.
7. "Who can control his fate?" Othello asks. Does Othello have any control over his own fate?
8. Discuss the significance of night settings in almost every scene of the play. In what ways is it a 'story of the night'?
9. Desdemona, Emilia and Bianca are seen by their menfolk as either possessions to be hoarded, problems to be managed, or offenders

to be punished. How do Desdemona, Emilia and Bianca present us with contrasting views of women in relation to men (and to each other) in this play?

10 Do you have any sympathy for Roderigo? Discuss the character, paying attention to his attitudes and values, expressed in his speeches.

Vocabulary for writing on *Othello*

Abroad: About; at large.

Beseech: Beg; request.

Chide: Criticise.

Conceit: An idea or thought; a literary term for an extended metaphor.

Cuckold: A man whose wife has been adulterous.

Knave: A troublemaker, someone who plays tricks; can be used affectionately to mean a joker.

Moor: A north-African Muslim.

Thou: You (formal).

Thee: You (informal).

Thy: Your.

Analysing a sample topic

Iago says: "The Moor is of a free and open nature". Does this explain why Iago is able to deceive Othello so easily?

Look at the question closely. Basically it is asking: Does Othello's naivety make him an easy target for Iago's plots? This seems easy but is quite a difficult question to answer.

- You need to know details. Remember that the audience hears and sees things characters don't, often because Iago makes sure that his victims stay uninformed. That would be a good introduction to the essay and the first thing to point out.
- Iago's victims can only judge him by what they hear and see or know about his behaviour. No matter how (dis)trusting of him Othello, or any other character for that matter, might be, he ensures that they can't compare notes – do you remember how he keeps Cassio away

from Othello during Othello's epileptic fit (4.1) and makes sure that Roderigo doesn't get anywhere near Desdemona by stressing that he, Iago, is the essential go between?

Sample introduction

Iago is perhaps one of the most evil characters ever created by Shakespeare. However, it is his uncanny ability to read human nature coupled with his complete disregard for others that assists him in carrying out his evil plans. The fact that the once 'valiant Othello' – Iago's opposite – is easily deceived by Iago can be attributed to both his 'free and open nature' and his hubris, but also to Iago's ability to perceive and use these personality traits to his own advantage. Furthermore, we must be aware that Iago manipulates almost every other character in the play, thus suggesting that even those with less 'open' natures than Othello are also deceived by his 'honest' facade. This combination of gullibility and evil manipulation helped along by fate explains Othello's tragic deception at the hands of evil.

Body paragraph 1

- Trace Othello's trajectory of decline from the beginning to the end of the play.
- Establish Othello's virtues and how his strength of character becomes a weakness in the hands of Iago, who is able to see the opportunity for manipulation.
- Examine Iago's deception of other characters, including Roderigo, Cassio and even his own wife, Emilia.

Body paragraph 2

- Contrast Othello's and Iago's character. Look at how Iago is able to convince Othello of his honesty.
- Expand on the specific weakness of Othello's faith in human nature: that it leaves him unable to compromise.
- Refer to quotes to highlight Iago's abilities for deception, 'I am not what I am', and to demonstrate Othello's blindness to reason in his continued use of the term 'honest Iago'.

Body paragraph 3

- Indicate the potential consequences of Othello's bravery.
- Explain the negative connotations which accompany Othello's sense of confidence. Examine how clearly his success causes resentment and jealousy in those around him.
- Question whether or not Othello is a calculating risk-taker, or simply as direct and honest as he appears. When declaring his marriage with the words 'That I have ta'en away this old man's daughter / It is most true: true I have married her' his brazen announcement could have caused such offence that it may have cost him his life, rather than winning over the hostile crowd.

Sample conclusion

The play's tragic conclusion cannot be completely explained by Othello's trusting nature. Although his simple emotions and quick temper make him more susceptible to Iago's plan than he otherwise may have been, Iago is an intellectually formidable villain. Not valuing anything besides revenge, he is not susceptible to the emotions that weaken other characters in the play. The utter precision with which he engineers Othello's downfall, combined with Othello's natural vulnerabilities, leaves Othello with little hope of escape.

SAMPLE ANSWER

"Who can control his fate?" Othello asks. Does Othello have any control over his own fate?

In order to ascertain Othello's own contribution to his demise, other forces must be taken into account. Firstly, there is the nature of a society that, in Iago's words, perceives him as an 'erring barbarian' and is quick to judge a man who is 'rude' in his speech and a 'Moor' besides. Secondly, Othello is inherently flawed, so that Iago's insidious words about Desdemona's preference for a match 'of her own clime, complexion, and degree' reinforce in Othello's mind the inferiority of his position in Cyprus or Venice, despite his status as a general. Ultimately a combination of Iago's intelligence in playing on Othello's insecurities ('look to your wife'), his inspired manipulation of events, Othello's own character and fate seem to work against Othello and bring about his downfall.

It could be construed that, rather than fate, the flaws in the characters around Othello lead to the play's terrible finale. Emilia's flaw is her misguided loyalty to Iago, demonstrated by her gift to Iago of the handkerchief that her 'wayward husband hath a hundred times wooed [her] to steal'. It is a trifle that causes Othello to yield to 'tyrannous hate' and perform an act that he atones for in suicide. In the same way, Desdemona's passivity and consequent failure to defend herself effectively against Othello's accusations perpetuate Othello's belief that she is a 'lewd minx'. Also, Othello's 'free and open nature' leads him to accept Iago's vile insinuations without much question. The seed of doubt planted in Othello's mind when Iago first voices his 'suspicions' bears fruit, as Othello soon laments 'the curse of marriage'.

The omen voiced by Brabantio in Venice could perhaps be seen as evidence of Othello's destiny; nothing he does will succeed in changing it. Desdemona's father cautions Othello that 'she [Desdemona] has deceived her father, and may thee' and from this early stage we are forewarned of the disaster to follow. Another such omen is the storm at the beginning of Act 2, which brings its own danger to the characters. Othello is separated from Desdemona and his friends by a 'foul and violent tempest', a storm which pre-empts another: Othello's unquenchable wrath, leading him to vow to 'tear [Desdemona] all to pieces!' Othello's anger will rage unchecked and spiral out of control until he commits the act which dooms him, murdering his 'soul's joy'. Othello also comments, 'when I love thee [Desdemona] not, chaos is come again', and this is truly what happens when Othello allows his 'black vengeance' to arise from its 'hollow cell'.

It is tempting to view Othello not as an individual, but as a figure representing all that is good and honourable in man, coupled with man's capacity for jealousy and revenge. This is the human condition. This perception leads to a foretold conclusion, as Othello is 'fated' to grapple with his emotions. His self-doubt wars with his wounded pride, causing him to farewell forever 'the tranquil mind'. Othello's flawed character renders him too quick to look to others for advice and too hasty by far to condemn Desdemona. 'Haply, for I am black, and have not those soft parts of conversation ... I am declined into the vale of years', he says. Othello is so insecure that he sees immediately all the reasons Desdemona might have forsaken him, rather than the truth of her love for her 'dear Othello'.

The unfair and highly limiting manner in which Othello treats Desdemona can be seen to contribute to the bloody final outcome. Although Othello could not have known about the extent of Iago's ambitions, he may have been able to prevent his own and Desdemona's deaths by adjusting his attitude towards Desdemona. From the beginning, his attitude towards Desdemona is based on objectification. Although he loves her, frequently calling her 'sweeting' and other terms of endearment, he ultimately does not respect her enough to trust her word against Iago's. Because Othello sees Desdemona as a possession rather than a human being, he lacks sufficient knowledge of her personality to accurately judge Iago's accusations against her. Othello's limited perspective increases his paranoia about his wife, as well as making him feel that he has the right to be able to physically dominate her. Although the play still could have ended tragically if Othello had had a greater measure of respect for, and more knowledge of, Desdemona, he may have been able to sidestep the fate that seemed inevitable.

While Othello does have control over his fate, the manner in which events work against him, and the treacherous actions of Othello's 'honest creature' Iago, set in motion a series of events from which Othello is unable to deviate. His role in the catastrophic finale does not seem to be preordained. One cannot help but feel one word from Desdemona could have averted the tragedy, yet instead she is condemned as a 'strumpet'. Othello's pride, in demanding Desdemona's death as payment for her 'infidelity', tells against him, as do his inherent character flaws. All of these factors contribute to the 'bloody period' that takes the lives of Desdemona, Emilia, Othello and Roderigo.

REFERENCES & READING

Text

Shakespeare, William, *Othello*, The New Penguin Shakespeare, Penguin Books, Harmondsworth, England, 1968, revised 1996.

Further reading

Abrams, M.H., *A Glossary of Literary Terms*, Austin, Texas, Holt, Rinehart & Winston, 1988.

Bradley, A.C., *Shakespearean Tragedy,* London, Macmillan (1904) from 1963 Lectures V and VI on *Othello,* 142–198.

Bullough, Geoffrey (ed. and *Introduction*), *Narrative and Dramatic Sources of Shakespeare,* Volume VII, *Othello,* 193–265, London, Routledge and Kegan Paul, 1973.

Crichton, A.B., 'Hecate's Watery Moon as a Guide to Othello's Imagination', *Shakespeare Studies*, 27, 1991.

Davison, Peter, *Othello: An Introduction to the Variety of Criticism*, The Critics Debate series, London, Macmillan, 1988.

Fiedler, Leslie A., 'The Moor as Stranger', in *The Stranger in Shakespeare,* UK, Paladin, 1974, 115–164.

Gutierrez, N.A., 'Witchcraft and Adultery in Othello: Strategies of Subversion' in Brink, Jean R. et al. *Playing with Gender: A Renaissance Pursuit*, Urbana and Chicago, University of Illinois Press, 1991.

Holloway, J., *The Story of the Night: Studies in Shakespeare's Major Tragedies*, London, Routledge & Kegan Paul, 1961 and USA, University of Nebraska Press, 1981.

Loomba, Ania, 'Sexuality and Racial Difference', in *Gender, Race, Renaissance Drama*, Manchester, Manchester University Press, 1989.

Marienstras, R., 'Othello, or the husband from afar' in *New Perspectives on the Shakespearean World*, New York, Cambridge University Press, 1985.

Muir, Kenneth (ed.), 'Essays on Rymer (Alexander) and Iago (Scragg)', *Shakespeare Survey 21*, Cambridge University Press, 1968.

Newman, Karen, '"And wash the Ethiop white": femininity and the monstrous in *Othello*', in Jean E. Howard & Marion F. O'Connor (eds.) *Shakespeare Reproduced: The Text in History and Ideology*. New York and London, Methuen, 1987.

Quarshie, Hugh, *Second Thoughts about Othello*, Occasional Paper No 7, International Shakespeare Association, Chipping Campden, England, 1999.

Rosenberg, M., *The Masks of Othello*, Berkley, California University Press, 1961.

Snyder, Susan, *Othello – Critical Essays*, New York and London, Garland, 1988.

Spencer, T.J.B., 'The Story of Disdemona of Venice and the Moorish Captain' in *Elizabethan Love Stories*, Penguin, 1968, pp.197.

Spivack, Bernard, *Shakespeare and the Allegory of Evil*, Columbia University Press, 1958.

Storr, Anthony, 'Othello and the Psychology of Sexual Jealousy' in *Churchill's Black Dog and Other Phenomena of the Human Mind*, Glasgow, Fontana/Collins, 1989, Chapter 5.

Suzman, J., *Acting with Shakespeare: Three Comedies*, New York & London, Applause, 1996.

Vaughan, V. M. & Cartwright, K (eds.), *Othello: New Perspectives*, (Twelve new essays on the play), London, Rutherford: Fairleigh Dickinson University Press, 1991.

Wine, Martin L., *Othello – Text and Performance*, London, Macmillan, 1984.

Films

The Tragedy of Othello, Orson Welles' film version, 1952, 91 minutes. Video: Roadshow Entertainment.

Othello, A BHE production from the National Theatre of Great Britain stage production, 1965, starring Sir Laurence Olivier as Othello. Video: RCA, Columbia Pictures/Hoyts Video, c 1991.

Othello, produced and directed by Jonathan Miller, starring Anthony Hopkins as Othello, 2 videos, BBC Enterprises, 1994.

Othello, Oliver Parker film version, 1995, 124 minutes. Video: Columbia Tristar Home Video, 1998.

Animated text and video

Shakespeare, The Animated Tales, Othello, abridged by Leon Garfield, Heinemann Young Books, London, and video by Shakespeare Animated Films/Christmas Films, 1994.